PRAISE FOR GAI

GW00470798

"Emotional and brilliant..."

— All About Romance

"Tastefully erotic ... more smart than smutty..."

— Publishers Weekly

"Powerful and compelling..."

— Foreword Reviews

REDEMPTION

A DARKEST SKIES NOVEL

GARRETT LEIGH

Edits: Posy Roberts @ Boho Edits

Cover Art: Garrett Leigh @ Black Jazz Design

Proofing: Con Riley, Annabelle Jacobs, Alex Korent

FOREWORD

For my non-Brit readers, some clarification of the dialogue you'll read in *Redemption*. *Road men/man*, *waste men/man*, *mash men/man* are all street talk for gang members, particularly in London and the south east. If someone is "on the road," they're in a gang, and/or engaged in gang activity. Perhaps the closest American equivalent is "in the game." And of course, street language is forever fluid. If you're reading this ten years after publication, the terminology will have likely moved on.

Also, you may notice there's no accent on the word cafe. This isn't a mistake. This is because in working class parts of any British city, particularly in the south, a greasy-spoon breakfast establishment, even if it says *cafe* on the sign outside, is universally pronounced *caff*. If you don't believe me, watch *Eastenders*.

1

Six years. Seventy-two months. 2190 days.

"That's it, Pope. You're done."

Luis blinked. "That's it?"

The guard with the kind face nodded. "Through that door and to the gate. Someone will let you out."

Dazed, Luis took the envelope he was offered and followed the guard's directions. The corridor was nondescript and smelt of bleach. *It's like a horror film. Someone's gonna bust me at the other end.* But there was no one waiting at the gate. In Luis's dreams, he'd pictured this moment with a bunch of keys and a surly guard begrudgingly setting him free. In reality, the gate was remotely operated and swung open as he approached.

The dodgy corner of London he'd once called home sprawled out before him. Betting shops, green grocers, empty premises where the Jewish butcher had once been. So familiar, yet so alien that he stopped in his tracks, stone cold, feet rooted to the concrete.

He shoved the envelope in his pocket and took a shuddery breath. Car fumes and the stink of the bins from the fried chicken shop reached him. He closed his eyes, and a deeper breath brought him the scent of the pie shop, despite the fact it had closed down before his trial, and the chip shop that served the best saveloys in town. It smelt like the past, and the future.

Whether he wanted it to or not, it smelt like home.

Luis opened his eyes and swept his gaze from the cracked pavement to the sky. Moss Farm loomed over the streets. Tower blocks, grimy from the day they were built, stood tall in the city, covered in a thousand grubby fingerprints. They cast shadows in every direction, metaphorically, at least, and their ominous gloom caught Luis off guard. Somehow he'd remembered them as something they weren't. Long, dark nights spent recalling the bright and colourful world he'd left behind. A world that didn't exist and never had.

Idiot. How had he forgotten this shithole? Grey, dull, and, in this neighbourhood, full of dickheads who'd have his wallet from his pocket if he didn't keep his head down. Two postcodes south, no fucker would meet his eye without respect. But respect came at a price, and Luis had the discharge grant in his pocket to prove it. Forty-six quid. He tried not to think about the piles of cash he'd left in his old flat. Dante would've had it away. Luis's brother looked out for himself. *Prick.*

The gate behind Luis swung shut. Metal scraped concrete. He rubbed his left ear as the sound reverberated in his tired brain, merging with the last words the prison doctor had said to him a month before his release. "*Don't forget to register with a GP. They can help you find an otolaryngologist.*"

Luis wondered if she realised she'd never told him what she meant, and even if he'd owned a phone, he couldn't spell the longest word in the world to google it. Probably not. Their meeting had lasted six minutes. One for every year he'd spent behind bars. Six minutes for seventy-two months of incarceration. *And you deserved every fucking day of it.*

"Come on, Pope. Get moving or we'll have you back in."

Startled, Luis glanced over his shoulder. A cluster of screws were eyeballing him from the watch point, laughing, sneering, the things the old Luis—the one who'd roamed the streets, all temper and no common sense—would've vaulted the gate to destroy. Prison Luis had learned to rein it in, to play the grey man and hope that life moved on without him.

He turned back to the outside world and stepped forwards with no real idea of where he was going. A housing charity had secured him a bedsit away from his old haunts, but he'd forgotten how to get there. If he'd ever known. It had been a long time since he'd last caught a bus. Counting back the years occupied him as he drifted away from the prison and into town. Some said he'd been lucky to be locked up so close to home, but as he approached the high street, he didn't feel lucky. *Cursed, more like.* Walking out to a place he'd never been would've meant a fresh start. A clean slate. And a reputation no fucker cared about. Here, every step felt like the life sentence he'd managed to avoid, and his legs felt like lead. The pavement turned to quicksand, dragging him down. Anxiety turned to panic, and the crisp winter air stung his throat.

Winter. Fuck. The last time he'd paid attention it had been high summer. The solitary tree in the exercise yard had been bright green and lush, the only slash of nature among men who'd forgotten how to live, and men who forgot that the seasons changed and in six long years hadn't bothered to ask the prison for a coat.

Shivering, Luis shifted his bag on his back and wrapped his arms around himself. Maybe the bus would be warm, but first, a trip to the job centre beckoned, followed by a check-in with a probation officer paid too little to give a shit, as long as he kept his nose clean. The few friends he'd made on the inside had told him to give it a couple of days. To get settled, get wasted, and get laid. But what was the point? He hadn't felt settled since the army men had come to the house on his fifth birthday, and the last person he'd fucked had been a road man, just like him.

He reached absently to the dog tags hanging around his neck, the sole personal possession the prison had handed back that morning. The warm metal against his cold hands grounded him, and he found the will to keep moving.

The job centre was on the high street. Inside, a security guard directed him to the waiting area. He said words, but Luis missed them. He took a seat, wishing he had a phone like everyone around him to pretend he had something to do. Time on his hands meant himself on his mind. *Fuck that shit.*

A man dropped into the seat beside him.

He smelt of weed and attitude. Luis studied the floor, but the sensation of being watched was hard to ignore. *Don't look.* Perhaps if he had, he'd have found the dude minding his own business and not giving a single fuck about Luis's paranoia. But he didn't look. He counted breaths, heartbeats, and stains on the carpet until his blood roared in his ears.

Luis sprang to his feet.

He booked it out of the building and crossed the road. New bars and pubs had opened since he'd last been here. He took a step towards one. Stopped. Changed his mind. Bars were crowded with idiots who wanted to fight. Luis didn't have the spoons for thug life anymore or the ears to cope with the noise.

Despair was like the flu. It crept up with mild symptoms, then impacted like a freight train. Luis's bag contained nothing but a pair of old jeans, sweatpants, and two T-shirts. It had seemed featherlight when he'd slung it on his back. Suddenly, it weighed a ton, and the bustle of the street boomed in his good ear, rattling his brain.

They'd warned him about this, on the inside. How the world had grown since he'd left it, and it would take time to acclimatise, but as a bus roared past and the market traders shouted above it, Luis couldn't see how he'd ever get used to this. Noise, colour, life. Inside, he'd craved it, but now he had it in abundance, it scared the shit out of him.

Calm your tits. He had two quid in his pocket, spare change he'd had when he'd been arrested. Back then, there'd been a cafe at the end of the road, hidden away behind the bank. Toni's. The same family had owned it for a million years, and if he closed his eyes—*in the middle of the street again like a total fucking moron*—Luis could hear the booming voice of the Italian granddad who'd served bucket-sized mugs of tea and doorstep sandwiches.

His stomach growled. He couldn't afford the sandwich, but god damn, he needed the tea.

The streets passed in a blur. Luis half expected to find the cafe had been turned into a hipster coffee bar, but it was there, in all its steamed-up window glory. He clutched the door handle like a drowning man. There was a sign on the glass panel, faded and blurred by condensation.

Help Wanted. Apply Within.

If it wasn't fate, it was the cruellest trick.

———

The door banged open. Paolo ignored it. If customers wanted his attention, they soon let him know. He kept his gaze on the two dozen rashers of bacon on the grill, flipped them, and cracked eight eggs into the frying pan to his left. Toast was the bane of his life. With a million other things to do, it was often the task that slipped by.

Or went horribly wrong.

The scent of burnt bread reached him. He lunged for

the toaster in time to rescue six carbonated squares of Hovis white sliced. "Fuck's sake."

Irritation spread through him, adding to the stress of what had already been a shitty day. And it was barely eleven. The lunchtime rush was still to come, and if it went anything like breakfast, it was going to be murder.

He spun around to hurl the bread in the bin. Fresh loaves were stacked on the counter. Consumed by the twelve orders on the pass, Paolo blurred there and back without glancing up, but a lifetime spent serving fry-ups to the good—and bad—people of the neighbourhood had left him attuned to the presence of someone waiting at the counter. "Be with you in a minute, mate."

No reply was forthcoming. Paolo shook his head. Idiot was probably lost in their phone, oblivious to the world around them like every other knobhead out there. *Who's got time for that shit?*

Paolo didn't. He loaded up a dozen plates, delivered them, and prepared himself to face whoever he'd kept waiting for ten minutes. *Have a pop. I dare you.*

He expected a tradesman or a hipster from the bank wanting "chai tea" when all Paolo stocked was Tetley, but as he reached the counter and finally looked up at the man flipping through the local rag, the six foot streak of brooding gorgeousness caught him off guard. *Wow.* This never happened.

Paolo had worked in the family cafe as long as he'd been able to walk and could count on one hand the fit blokes who'd walked in the door and turned his head. It was a sum total of two. Dante Pope and his younger brother Luis, but it had been a long time since either Pope brother had graced the high street. Rumour had it, Dante was running a county lines empire from his tower block apartment on Moss Farm while Luis Pope had been in prison for years. So long, Paolo had assumed he was never getting out and had forgotten all about him.

It's not him. It can't be.

But the more Paolo stared at the man at the counter, the harder it was to deny. Luis Pope had aged in the years he'd been gone, but fuck, if it hadn't made him hotter. Like fine wine, time had chiselled his boyish good looks. His shoulders had broadened, and his hair had grown out. Dark stubble covered his strong jaw, and beneath his thin T-shirt, his torso was a long, rippled line of sinewy strength. He was ... beautiful. Shame Paolo couldn't stand him. *Fucking waste man. What's he even doing in here?*

There was no way to find out without asking. Paolo wiped his hands on his apron. "What can I get you?"

Luis Pope kept his eyes on the newspaper, full bottom lip caught between his teeth, brows furrowed. Paolo wanted to punch him and rescue his pillowy lip in equal measure.

He settled for rapping his knuckled on the newspaper. "Hello?"

Luis flinched. It was infinitesimal, and his jaw set a split second later, but Paolo saw it and filed it away in the *what the fuck* section of his brain. Luis Pope didn't flinch. In his day, a mere mention of his name had sent shivers down the spines of those who'd had cause to fear him. Too busy keeping the family business afloat, Paolo had never been one of them, but the Pope brothers were infamous. Gangsters, road men, whatever. Luis Pope was a name, not a man who startled so easily.

Paolo tried again. "What do you want?"

Luis gaze flicked to the chalkboards above Paolo's head. "Tea, please."

"Anything else?"

"A job if you still have it."

He'd have surprised Paolo less if he'd stripped naked and asked for a hand job. Paolo blinked. "What?"

"The job in the window," Luis said. "If it's still available, I'd like to apply."

"*You* want to wash dishes and bus tables?"

It was Luis's turn to blink. Shock coloured his hazel eyes, and a faint flush stained his cheeks. "Yeah, actually. I do, but if the position's been filled, I'll just take the tea."

The position had been vacant for the best part of a month, ever since Paolo's last staff member had deserted him to go to university. There'd been other applicants, but trial shifts hadn't gone well. Apparently, Paolo lacked the patience to train anyone to the standard needed to be of any use to him. And, according to the one who'd fled the cafe just yesterday, he was an arsehole.

A desperate arsehole who couldn't face another day running the cafe alone.

Still, there was a difference between desperate and stupid. However pretty Luis Pope was, he was trouble, always had been. And him asking for a job had to be some kind of sick joke.

Paolo took the two-pound coin Luis had dropped on the counter. "Take a seat. I'll bring the tea over."

He backed up without waiting for an answer and turned to the urn to fill an oversized mug with the strong tea the cafe was known for. He loaded the mug and a jug of milk onto a tray and took it to the table Luis had retreated to.

Luis didn't look up. Paolo dumped his wares on the table and walked away, but Luis's presence behind him smouldered like embers that could ignite at any moment, and only the stubbornness Paolo had inherited from his Nonna stopped him going back and demanding to know if Luis Pope was taking the royal piss.

The cafe was busy too—too busy for Paolo to waste his time throwing glances at the man hunched over his tea mug. He did it anyway, though, until a crowd of builders came in and fucked up his day. Six rounds of bangers and chips later, he searched out Luis again, but the table by the door was empty.

Luis Pope was gone.

2

"Don't be so harsh, boy. It doesn't become you."

Paolo scowled, but it was hard to maintain it under the stern gaze of his grandfather. The old dude's mobility was long gone, but Toni remained razor-sharp and was able to school Paolo with a simple frown. "I'm not being harsh. It's true, he's a road man. Always has been. I don't know why he was sniffing round our place, but it can't be anything good."

"I can't remember what a road man is, but if you say it, I believe it. I just think a man deserves a second chance. You said yourself, he's been gone a long time. Who's to say he's the same as he used to be?"

"What's to say he isn't?"

"Nothing. But if no one gives him a chance, that will never change. Your father was like that, in trouble for so long it seemed the only way. Perhaps if someone had given him a job when he was willing to ask for one, things might've been different."

The conversation went round in circles and back again to the point where Paolo wished he'd never mentioned Luis Pope, but Toni had always possessed a sixth sense, a nose for when something had got under Paolo's skin. He'd have dug it out of him eventually.

Paolo lost three games of draughts in a row, then caught the bus home. It stopped outside the corner shop. Paolo spent all day surrounded by food but often forgot to eat and fill his own kitchen cupboards with anything but ketchup and spaghetti hoops.

The shop sold every exotic spice he could think of, along with a million different fruit and veg that Paolo couldn't name. It smelt amazing but required brain power to prepare, something he was lacking after a twelve-hour stint in the cafe. He bought instant noodles and a packet of chocolate digestives. At the counter, he resisted the call of the cigarettes and picked up a bottle of rum instead. It would last longer. Probably. Maybe.

Outside, the autumn air had turned cold. He zipped his jacket and pulled his hood up, letting it hang low over his face to keep the wind out. His flat was a ten-minute walk away. One day he'd get round to cleaning out the studio above the cafe so he could live there, but that day wasn't today. Besides, who wanted to live at work?

Not me.

The wind kept his head down, past the homeless bedding down in shop doorways and the teens congregated outside McDonalds. Not that he'd have risked glancing around much anyway. The high street was a fucking theme park at night, and he'd had enough of people for one day.

He crossed the road by the bus stop. A lone figure sat in the shelter, huddled against the cold, arms wrapped around himself.

Strong arms, with gang tattoos and no coat.

Damn it. The Paolo that had rebuffed Luis Pope that morning would've paid little attention—*aside from ogling those fine arms*—but with Toni's words ringing in his ears, he slowed to a stop, despite every instinct he had screaming at him to walk on by.

Luis looked up as Paolo drew level with him. His eyes were hooded and tired, face drawn. He nodded his recognition and stretched long legs out in front of him.

Paolo leaned on the bus shelter and folded his arms. "When did you get out?"

"Out?"

"Yeah. I know who you are."

"That why you wouldn't give me a job?"

"There is no job."

"Why's the sign still up then?"

"I forgot to take it down."

Luis nodded again and went back to staring at the ground. Paolo straightened up and tried to make himself move. The one-in-a-million possibility that Luis wasn't who he'd thought he was had been dispelled, and his reasons for sending him packing still stood, but something kept him anchored in place. A pull in his gut he couldn't decipher. Luis Pope was nothing to him but a notorious name and a tired face. What did he care if he was washed up at a bus stop like he had nowhere to go?

I don't care.

It was true. And yet he didn't move. "Look," Paolo said. "I kinda thought you were taking the piss earlier, but if you're serious and you promise not to bring any of your gang bullshit to my door, maybe we can talk."

Luis said nothing.

Paolo sighed and turned away.

"Wait." Luis stood and ventured out of the bus shelter. "I'm not in a gang anymore. So if that's why you blanked me, it's not true."

"I thought you had to die to get out of your gang?"

Luis snorted. "Then you watch too much TV. I've been away for six years, and I don't talk to anyone from Moss Farm no more."

"What about your brother?"

"What about him? You see him anywhere round here? I'm waiting for the bus, man, to take me back to my shitty bedsit on Crawley road that I ain't got no Ps to pay for. Think about that before you judge me."

He stepped around Paolo and strode away. Startled, Paolo called after him. "What about your bus?"

Luis didn't answer.

———

Luis woke with a jump. For a moment, he lay still, legs tangled in second-hand sheets, and waited for the lights to come on. But nothing happened because he wasn't in his cell anymore, and if he wanted the lights on, he had to get out of bed and flick the switch his damn self.

Or maybe not, since he'd forgotten to buy tokens for the electric metre. And it was *cold* in the bedsit, something he'd rarely felt crammed into the overcrowded prison. He'd rarely been alone, too, and had spent long days and nights craving solitude, but now he had it, the shine had worn off. Trying to fall asleep in utter silence had made his heart race, like it had in the job centre. He'd worked out for hours to take the edge off, but all he'd gained was sore muscles and a dizzy spell that had sent him to his knees, his empty stomach heaving, crying out for the meals he'd missed since the prison gates had opened for him. Toni's tea had been magic: hot and sweet. Shame it had come at a price.

Shivering, he rolled over and wrapped the duvet the housing charity had provided tighter around himself. The mattress on the divan bed was lumpy and old, but a world away from the padded shelf he'd slept on in prison. *You should be grateful.* And he was. Didn't make his current situation any easier to swallow, though. The charity had fronted him a month's rent. After that, he was on his own, and if the kid from Toni's reaction to him was anything to go by, getting a job in the neighbourhood was going to be tough.

And the dude fronting Toni's was hardly a kid. Tall and lean, he was the kind of man Luis had spent his entire adult life fantasising about. Dark hair, dark eyes, and strong, capable hands. Luis had watched him work in the cafe, taking orders, cooking, and cleaning tables like a one-man machine, and it had lit something in him he hadn't felt in a long time. Attraction. Desire. And crushing disappointment when recognition had dawned in the other man's eyes and his derision had kicked Luis in the nuts.

Luis closed his eyes, hoping to ward off the reminder, but all he got for his trouble was a flashback of their second encounter at the bus stop, and it was too early—or late—for that shit.

He gave up on sleep and swung his legs out of bed. The carpet felt strange against his bare feet. He dug socks from his bag and took two steps into what constituted his kitchen—a tiny breakfast bar, a fridge, a hob, and solitary cupboard. The washing machine was in the bathroom, keeping the shower cubicle company. It was the most space he'd had all to himself in as long as he could remember, and it somehow managed to be both awesome and horrible at the same time.

The charity had furnished the kitchen with a kettle, a toaster, and enough crockery and cutlery for one miserable person. All he needed was food, but the forty-six pounds he'd tucked in the cupboard last night felt too precious to spend. *You need to go back to the job centre and sign on.* True facts, but after yesterday, he'd rather starve. Or at least hold out a little longer.

He took a shower without looking over his shoulder. The gas-powered hot water lasted fifteen minutes before it started to give out. Skin flushed from the heat, he dressed in the same jeans, and another thin T-shirt. He'd planned on staying home until businesses started to open, but with nothing for company, save his own thoughts, agitation swept over him. Lack of routine made his skin crawl, the quiet, the freedom. *I gotta get out of here.*

Luis left the bedsit. Outside it was cold and barely light, but enough people were up and about to make the world seem real.

He paced the pavements, tracking past the park, the petrol station, and towards the cash-and-carry store at the end of the road. The fresh air felt amazing against his bare skin, and he almost didn't notice the biting cold.

Almost. *Man, it's fucking freezing.*

"Still no coat, eh?"

Luis jumped and swung his gaze sideways. For the second time in twenty-four hours, the man from Toni's had walked up on him, this time from the exit door of the cash-and-carry. *Jesus, what are the chances?*

Not that it mattered. Despite the dude being glorious to look at, he was the last person on earth Luis wanted to see.

One of them, at least.

Luis turned away and kept walking, figuring the bloke was already bored with whatever conversation he'd been trying to start, but found his path blocked by six foot of scowling Italian. "Fuckin-A, mate. What do you *want*?"

"What do I want?" The man raised his hands as if considering putting them on Luis—*let him try*—then seemed to change his mind. "I thought it was you who wanted a job?"

Luis shrugged, his stance as non-combative as he could

bear. He'd learnt to be painfully neutral in prison, pleasant enough to be liked, quiet enough to stay under the radar. With no Moss Farm boys on the wing, it had worked, but out here where his face was known, looking weak was a risk. His hands itched to push the man away, a warning, and the only one he'd get.

He balled them into fists and shoved them in his pockets. "Yeah, well. It was *you* who told me it didn't exist, so why are you up in my face again?"

The man glanced over his shoulder. "I spoke to my granddad. He seems to think we need the help enough to put up with whatever trouble you bring to our door."

"I already told you I don't run with the Moss Farm boys anymore."

"When did you get out?"

"Yesterday."

"What are you doing roaming the streets at five in the morning?"

"What do you care?"

It was the other man's turn to shrug. "I don't care if you're just out for a morning stroll, but if you're on your way home from something dodgy, this conversation's over."

"I didn't ask you for this conversation." Luis kept his voice low, swallowing the frustration expanding in his chest. How was this even his life? He'd dreamt about cafe dude, but not like this. Never once had he imagined him becoming so fucking annoying. "If you don't want to have it anymore, let me pass."

"I didn't say that."

"Then what are you saying? Because as much as I've got nowhere else to be, I haven't got time for this."

"Do you have time to work today?"

Luis glanced up sharply. "What?"

"Work. As in, work for me. Today. I'm snowed under and could do with the help if you're up for a trial shift."

The sun broke through the clouds behind the train line, grey streaked with a golden glow. Tension bled from Luis's shoulders. "What's your name?"

"Why does that matter?"

"I want to know if you're serious."

"How does knowing my name help you with that?"

"You know mine."

"That's not my fault."

Luis couldn't deny it. But stubbornness flowed through him thicker than blood. He'd mellowed in the six years he'd spent with no choices or autonomy, but without rhyme or reason, the world had stopped turning until the beautiful man in front of him revealed his name.

"Paolo."

"Paolo what?"

"Cilberto. Like my granddad, Toni."

"I know him. Big guy with the giant moustache."

"That's the one." A faint smile brightened the man's— brightened *Paolo's* face. "He hasn't run the cafe in years, though, so why he thinks he's got a say in who I hire, I have no fucking clue."

"And yet here we are."

"Here we are," Paolo agreed. "Now, do you want the job or not?"

GARRETT LEIGH

"I want it."

"Can you start now?"

"Now?"

"You said you had nowhere else to be."

Luis spread his hands. "Then I guess I'm all yours."

3

Paolo led Luis to the loaded trolley he'd wheeled out of the cash-and-carry. "Delivery didn't come in, so I've got to hoof all this back to the cafe."

"Where's your car?"

"Don't have one."

Luis nodded as if a trolley stacked high with eggs, bacon, and sausages and no way of taking it anywhere made perfect sense. "It's a long walk."

"It is. I'm waiting for an Uber."

"Oh."

Paolo laughed. "Did you think we were gonna pack up like donkeys and walk?"

"You said hoof it. I took you literally."

In another world, Luis Pope could've taken Paolo any way he wanted, but they weren't in another world. They were in this one. The one where Paolo had just idiotically hired a gang banger to bus his tables and had been so eager to do so, he'd left the cash-and-carry store without packing his goods into bags.

Luis noticed his mistake first. He gestured to the bags hanging unused on the handle bars. "Want me to put this stuff in those?"

"If you want."

Luis unhooked the bags and began loading them with packets of bacon and sausages. Paolo should've helped but stood back and watched instead, letting his gaze, and thoughts, run riot as Luis worked.

He looked exactly the same as he had yesterday, and yet Paolo could tell he was a different man. His first night of freedom had changed him, and Paolo wondered why. Luis hadn't divulged what he was doing out and about at the crack of dawn, but the bedsit he'd revealed yesterday wasn't far away. Perhaps he really had been out for a morning stroll.

Yeah, right. Suspicion warred with Toni's wise words. Paolo joined Luis at the trolley and reached for the eggs. "Aren't you going to ask me how much I'm going to pay you?"

Luis glanced up. He frowned, and confusion flashed in his eyes so briefly Paolo thought he'd imagined it. "Is it more than the dole?"

"I think it's called universal credit these days, but yeah, it'll be more than that."

"Then I don't care how much it is as long as I can pay my rent."

"How much is your rent?"

"Six hundred quid."

Paolo raised an eyebrow. That was cheap for the city.

"It's subsidised," Luis elaborated, clearly reading his mind. "Through the charity that works with the prison. I can only stay twelve months, though. Then I have to find somewhere else."

Even in this shitty neighbourhood, he was going to struggle to find anywhere close to six hundred quid on the wage Paolo could afford to pay him, but Paolo figured he already knew that. Sky-high housing costs weren't a new thing, though it likely wasn't something Luis Pope had worried about when he was slinging drugs out of the Moss Farm tower blocks all those years ago. *If* that was what he'd been doing. Back then, the Pope brothers had been feared for all kinds of things—drugs, knives, guns. Paolo had never been interested enough to care what was true. *And I don't care now.*

They packed up the produce and the Uber car appeared to carry them the ten-minute drive back to the cafe. Time was getting on. Paolo had a lot to do before he opened the doors at six.

Inside, he directed Luis to the fridges to pack the meat products away. "Eggs go on the shelves in the back room. Don't drop them. I haven't got time to fetch any more."

Luis didn't answer, but Paolo was fast growing used to that. It was as if he only heard the things he wanted to and completely blocked out what he didn't. *All right for some.*

Paolo flew around the cafe, thankful his grandparents had instilled in him the habit of closing down properly every night. Everything was where it should've been. Even the sauce bottles were full and ready.

He lit the grill and fired up the tea urn. Loaded the bread baskets and counted the float in the till. There wasn't much there, fifty quid, maybe more. Pennies to most people, but with nursing home fees to pay, it meant the world to Paolo. What would he tell Toni if Luis turned out to be casing the place for his crew? If he came back tomorrow morning to find it all gone?

The ridiculousness of it left Paolo shaking his head. Of all the businesses the Moss Farm gang could turn over, Toni's Cafe was hardly prize pickings. What were they going to do? Flog Formica tables from the back of their mopeds?

Not that any gang member with Luis's standing rode a moped. Nah. The top boys cruised the streets in blacked-out Audis, there for all the world to see, and yet invisible at the same time. Sometimes they drove up and down the high street, slow and steady, music rumbling so deep it made the cafe windows shake. Paolo had never paid them much attention, but he couldn't help wondering if they'd come looking for Luis one day. *They're not coming in my place.* But the truth was, there was little Paolo could do to stop them, and more doubts swept over him, settling with the conflict already raging in his gut. Toni had counselled to give Luis a chance, and fate had crossed their paths twice since then. But what about common sense? What about the logic screaming that Luis Pope was nothing but trouble?

"What time do you open?"

"Hmm?" Paolo startled, frozen with ten slices of bread in each fist. "What?"

Luis took a step closer, then seemed to change his mind. "It's six o'clock and there's people outside. I was wondering when you open."

Paolo threw a glance at the clock on the wall. Six o'clock. *Shit.* He dumped the bread in the baskets and reached for his apron. The keys were by the till. He tossed them to Luis. "We open now. Unlock the door, will you?"

Luis sloped off to the door. He unlocked it and held it open for the first customers of the day. He hadn't looked at Paolo much since their first encounter the day before, but it was hard to miss the way his gaze slid to the floor as the early birds filed in. His hair fell over his face, hiding the chiselled good looks and mean mug that made him look like the road man Paolo judged him to be. For a moment, he seemed to shrink into himself, and an odd urge to cross the cafe and brush his hair back swept over Paolo, a prickly heat that made his skin tingle. *What the actual fuck? I need coffee, man. I'm losing my mind.*

Paolo retreated to the grill. Luis joined him. "What do you need me to do?"

"Bus tables, rinse stuff and stick it in the dishwasher. Clean anything that gets dirty."

"That's it? Who's going to serve and cook?"

"Me."

"All of it?"

"Yeah. Don't worry, I'm used to it."

Luis didn't seem worried. If anything, he looked relieved, but there was no time to ponder it. A line formed at the till. Paolo took orders as fast as he could manage and lined them up over the grill. Bacon hit the hot bars, sausages sizzled over the flames, and the scent of Toni's famous fried breakfast filled the cafe. The hours flew by. Luis bussed tables like a pro while Paolo grilled too many rashers of bacon to count and didn't burn a single slice of toast. *I could get used to this.*

Around eleven, the breakfast rush died off. Paolo made two final plates of food and carried one out the back to where Luis was working the dishwasher. "Take a break."

Luis didn't answer.

Paolo sighed and tapped him on the shoulder. "Take a—"

Luis whirled round, arms raised. His elbow connected with the plate and set it flying across the room.

It clattered into the wall. Egg yolk and plate fragments slid down the old paint in slow motion, and it took a second for Paolo to realise Luis's elbow had been meant for his face. "The fuck?"

He shoved Luis back. Luis hit the dishwasher with a metallic thud, and a spark lit his eyes. Anger. But in a split second, it was gone, and horror replaced rage. His gaze darted between Paolo and the broken plate, and he cringed. "Shit. I'm so sorry. I didn't hear you coming."

"How could you not hear me coming?" Paolo snapped. "It's not a fucking nightclub in here, and there's like, three customers out front."

"Sorry." Luis stepped around Paolo. He bent to retrieve the broken plate, gathering the pieces with shaky hands. The tendons in his neck stood out. Everything about him screamed distress, and Paolo was struck by a sudden certainty that *he* was the one who'd fucked up.

He took a step forwards, but a customer called for attention.

Cursing, he dashed for the service counter and threw together the quickest bacon sandwich known to man. He served it up and returned to the kitchen, but there was no sign of the broken plate or the mess it had made. Luis was at the dishwasher, loading plates like nothing had happened.

Lacking any better ideas, Paolo left him to it.

————

The cafe shut at four, but it was barely three when Paolo came to find Luis to tell him he was done for the day.

Luis eyed the cleaned dishes that still needed to be put away. "What about those?"

"I'll do them. To be honest, I wasn't expecting you to get so much done. I'm usually just starting to catch up by now."

Luis could believe it. The cafe did a roaring trade, and it was hard to imagine anyone could manage it on their own.

Paolo never stopped moving. If he wasn't cooking, he was serving, taking money, or doing the thousand other things that needed doing when no one was asking for food. And he did it all with a scowl and a sharp tongue. Paolo Cilberto was a moody motherfucker. All day long, he growled and swore, muttered under his breath, and kicked anything and everything that got in his way. It was something else to watch, but Luis had spent most of the day with his head down, especially after he'd elbowed a full plate of food across the kitchen.

Mortification burnt his cheeks. He washed his hands in the sink and considered making a break for it, but the masochist in him needed to face Paolo and find out if his mini meltdown had cost him his job.

He dried his hands on a tea towel and forced himself to step out of the relative safety of the kitchen. The cafe was quiet. Paolo was sitting at a table in the corner, chewing on a pen as he frowned at some paperwork.

Luis shuffled over. "I'll be off, then, unless you need anything else?"

"Are you coming back tomorrow?" Paolo didn't look up as he spoke, but it felt like a trick question.

To answer yes was presumptuous, but anything else would make Luis seem like he didn't give a shit. "Um, if you want me to?"

"You're taking the piss, right?" Paolo dropped his pen on the table and swept his arm around the cafe. "I told you, this time most days I'm crying into the sink. I haven't looked at the accounts in months. If you can show up a few days a week and give me a break from that, the job's yours."

"For real?"

"For real. I mean, we need to talk numbers and shit, and I don't have time for that right now, but I can give you a call later so you can make your mind up?"

Luis's heart sank. "I don't have a phone."

"Why not?"

Because the one I had six years ago is rotting in an evidence vault somewhere, and I don't have the money to buy another one. "Haven't got round to it yet."

Paolo's dark eyes narrowed, and he tilted his head sideways, studying Luis hard enough to make Luis squirm before he seemed to reconcile with whatever he was thinking.

He pushed his chair back with a screech that rattled Luis's ears and disappeared into the kitchen. The minutes ticked by. Luis considered slipping out the front door and never coming back. He needed a job, but Paolo made him feel strange. One moment Luis was lost in his dark beauty, the next he was embarrassing himself over a plate of egg on toast.

Luis shuddered, the sound of the plate hitting the wall echoing in his head. In a world he didn't hear enough of anymore, *fuck*, he'd heard that. Felt it too, in the pit of his stomach, as the food had splatted on the floor. It had been thirty-one hours and counting since he'd last eaten. Risking his precious cash on supplies depended on him getting a job.

On *keeping* a job.

With a heavy sigh, he dropped into a nearby chair just as Paolo emerged from the kitchen.

Paolo returned to his own seat and held out a battered phone. "You can borrow this if you like. Get yourself a SIM card from the Tesco Express down the road. You can get them preloaded with credit for a fiver. Text me the number later, and I'll give you a call."

"You're lending me a phone?"

"I am. But it's a piece of shit, so if you decide not to come back, you can bin it."

Luis hadn't held a phone in years. Inside, some prisoners had them smuggled in, but he'd tried to avoid those faces, even the ones Dante had instructed him to watch over. Luis rubbed subconscious fingers over the scar above his left ear. He'd grown his hair out to hide it, but sometimes it throbbed and burned like the devil had been stitched into his skull.

He took the phone Paolo held out, a foil-wrapped package, and the scrap of paper scrawled with a phone number. Paolo's phone number. Of all the ways Luis had dreamt of scoring Paolo's digits the previous night, none were the charity handout this was turning out to be.

The foil package was warm and smelt of bacon. Luis's head spun. "What is it?"

"Bacon and egg bap. I made you one earlier, but you threw it at my head."

"Sorry about that."

Paolo shrugged. "Whatever. It was only a plate. Just do me the courtesy of letting me know if you're not interested in the job, okay? I've got better shit to do than chase you."

Luis nodded and took his cue to disappear. He tucked the phone and the scrap of paper in his pocket and made tracks. Outside, it had turned cold again and was already starting to get dark. Luis's T-shirt was damp from washing dishes, and the biting wind cut deep. Home was a bus ride away if he didn't fancy the cold walk—news flash, he didn't—but he'd left the bedsit that morning without his magic envelope. His only choice was to trudge his way back on foot, then head straight out again for a SIM card.

Thirty minutes later, he staggered inside with leaden legs, numb hands, and nipples that could cut glass. The by-now cold sandwich called his name, but a hot shower came first. Clean and defrosted, he devoured the bap Paolo had made him in two bites. It was the nicest thing he'd ever eaten. Real food hit his stomach like a warm hug, and he lay back on the bed, tempted by sleep. A cocoon of fatigue enveloped him. He shuffled under the covers and closed his eyes before he remembered the phone, the SIM card, and Paolo's phone number.

Crawling out of bed felt like sacrilege, but Paolo's number called to him like a beacon. He loaded the SIM card and turned the phone on. It was fully charged, and the home screen was a picture of the burly old man Luis remembered as Toni, smiling, with his arm around a dainty woman who had Paolo's flinty smile. The phone-book had six contacts, all Italian, but none of them Paolo. Luis typed in the number from the scrap of paper and saved it.

"Text me the number and I'll give you a call."

It sounded so simple, and it was, but something about Paolo terrified Luis more than any road man he'd ever faced. Not because of anything he did, but for how his mere presence made Luis's heart thump and blood rush. *That shit ain't normal.*

But what was normal? In this brave new world, Luis had no idea.

He tapped out a message.

this is my number, Luis Pope

Then erased his surname as if he could scratch it from history, or at least from the memories Paolo clearly had of him. He pictured his world six, eight, ten years ago. Perhaps they'd been at school together. Sat next to each other in class, but Luis didn't remember because he'd lived a lifetime since then, and the boy he'd been was nothing like the washed-up piece-of-shit man he'd become. Still, the possibility that Paolo had once been in his life and he'd been too distracted by slinging to notice *burned*. Paolo had looks that stopped traffic. How engrossed did a man need to be to not see him?

Luis stared at the phone for a full ten minutes, resisting the urge to scroll through the old messages and social media accounts, all the while pondering who the phone had belonged to. The lack of contacts saved pointed to someone old, but then, Luis could count on one hand the people he'd want saved in his own imaginary phone. A sum total of zero. He was twenty-seven years old and a total billy no mates.

Paolo didn't reply. Luis shoved the phone under his pillow and closed his eyes. A nap seemed a world away now, and he had shopping to do, but Paolo's silence bothered him. What if he'd had second thoughts? What if he'd inspected the pots and pans Luis had cleaned and found them not clean enough? Luis's discharge grant was supposed to last until he got paid from employment or a dole cheque came through, whatever they were calling it these days. Either way, if Paolo had changed his mind, that money would have to last weeks.

Sleep cost nothing. Luis tried to quiet his mind and take himself back to the only normal he could remember. The snoring and fidgeting of three other men replaced the silence of the bedsit. The mattress beneath him hardened, and the worn duvet cover became a scratchy blanket. Cold faded to stuffy warmth. Racing thoughts slowed. Two days of stress and hard work caught the anxious beast and tamed it. Luis drifted in that sacred place between consciousness and sleep, enjoying the ride. He was so nearly there, then a tiny click from the hallway startled him back to the beginning.

Dazed, Luis sat up, half convinced the sound had come from his hazy imagination. If he hadn't sensed Paolo behind him, how on earth would he hear whatever his brain was telling him had come from the hallway?

It doesn't work like that, remember? They told you lots of different things affect what you can hear. Luis's good ear was nearest the door to the hallway. That, along with the knowledge he wouldn't sleep if he didn't, convinced him to get up and check.

A folded page from a newspaper lay on the floor beneath the letterbox. Luis stared at it, apprehension blooming in his gut, glad he still hadn't bought tokens for the electric metre. The front door was cheap and thin, with no window, but he crept towards the paper as if he had a thousand eyes on him. He picked it up and unrolled it. Another phone number greeted him, but the last one on earth he actually wanted.

Beneath it was a note.

Call me bro, D

A full-body shiver passed through Luis. He didn't bother to wonder how Dante had found him, but he'd been counting on it taking him a little longer. At least until he had a job he could point to as reason for why he couldn't re-join the family firm. Knowing Dante, it wouldn't have put him off for long, but by then, perhaps Luis might've had enough money to be somewhere else.

Somewhere far enough from the city that Dante couldn't be bothered to come looking for him. After all, it wasn't like he'd taken the trouble to visit Luis in prison. No one had. He'd been as alone then as he was now.

He took the phone number to the kitchen and tossed it in the empty fridge. Fury swept through him that he didn't have the balls to put it in the bin, but he'd never had balls when it came to Dante, and Dante knew it. He didn't give a single fuck about Luis—he was a tool to him, a puppet. Not a brother, but a pawn in a sick game Luis could never win.

You'll call him, though, won't you?

Of course he would. If he didn't, Dante would come banging on his door, inserting himself into the silent, safe space Luis had a chance to carve out in the shitty bedsit he called home.

He backed out of the kitchen and returned to the sanctuary his lumpy bed seemed when he compared it to standing in the draughty kitchen and glaring at the fridge. His heart beat louder, but not with the heat it did whenever he caught sight of Paolo. No. This was different. This was a fear he knew.

His borrowed phone vibrated somewhere on the bed.

Another shot of terror curdled his insides. *Seriously? He's stalking me enough to have this number?*

But that was impossible, even for Dante ...

Unless Paolo was working for him, and he'd offered Luis a job to keep him where Dante could find him. Dante was well capable of manipulating the world enough to get what he wanted, but the theory relied on him knowing that Luis would walk into Toni's—

Stop it. Luis sucked in a deep breath. For that to work, Paolo would've had to be faking his disgust for street bangers, and nothing on earth would've made Luis believe that shit was anything but bone-deep and real.

He found the phone halfway down the bed. A message lit up the screen, from Paolo.

got caught up and couldn't call. do u want to come back tomorrow?

Luis hesitated only a moment before he tapped out his reply.

yes.

4

yes.

Paolo opened the message a dozen times, as if each time he opened it would tell him something new about the man he didn't recognise as the Luis Pope he remembered.

Or thought he remembered. Truth be told, most of what he knew about the Pope brothers was based on rumours and rep. *Nasty* reps that still sounded warning bells every moment Paolo gave up to thinking about Luis, which was more than he cared to admit, especially at 4am, when he'd spent all night fielding updates from his nonna's nursing home.

Tired, he rolled out of bed and stumbled to the shower. Under the hot spray, Luis filled his mind again, but this time, not the horror in his eyes when he'd flung his breakfast across the room. Instead, his muscled back, hidden beneath his stretched T-shirt, and his beautiful forearms took over. Heat pooled at Paolo's groin. He shook his head, trying to clear it, but the images of Luis wouldn't quit. The man was a masterpiece. Even if Paolo never saw him again, he would forever be his ultimate fantasy.

So one day with OG Pope has ruined all men for me. Excellent.

The thought was galling enough for Paolo to ignore his morning wood. He showered his restless night away, dressed, and left the house under a cloud of misty dark sky. Sometimes, it was hard to believe a new day had begun when he left the house in the pitch black of the previous night. Winter made his shoulders sag and his legs feel heavy, but then summer months trapped indoors were a bitch too. *Fuck my life.*

He hadn't replied to Luis's affirmative message about taking the cafe job; drama at the nursing home had distracted him. His plan had been to message him when he'd downed his first cup of shitty instant coffee, but as he neared the end of the high street, a tall figure stepped out of the shadows, shivering in the frigid air.

Luis.

For some reason, the sight of him, cold and clearly as tired as Paolo, made Paolo want to cry. He settled for a grunt. "Morning. I was going to tell you to come in at six."

Luis shrugged—Paolo was coming to learn it was his baseline of communication. "Had to get electric from the shop, so I was awake. You don't have to pay me for the extra hour."

"We'll talk about that after coffee."

Luis said nothing. Paolo preceded him to the cafe door and opened up, stepping aside to let Luis pass. He was wearing different clothes, dark jogging bottoms and a grey

T-shirt, and his hair was damp from the shower. It was a hundred colours: dark brown, chestnut, and subtly streaked with gold. The kind of hair women paid a hundred quid for, but Luis had scored it for free.

It looked soft, like silk. Paolo itched to run his fingers through it. *Perv.* It felt like more than that, but he couldn't decipher the butterfly sensation in his gut. He was too damn tired. And perhaps that was it. Fatigue induced horniness. It was a thing, right?

Besides, no one in their sane mind wouldn't be attracted to Luis.

Paolo followed him inside, flipping the lights on as he went. The heating was already on, timed to perfection so Paolo never walked into a cold cafe, and as he watched Luis's broad shoulders drop and his shivers ease, he'd never been more glad of his poxy radiators.

He moved to the coffee machine and switched it on, giving more thanks to yesterday's Paolo who'd set it up for the first batch of the day. Luis hovered in the kitchen doorway. "What do you need me to do?"

"You can slice the mushrooms, tomatoes, and the black pudding in a minute, but I figured we'd get a coffee first and have the conversation we didn't get round to last night."

Luis nodded.

Paolo turned back to the coffee jug. "How do you take it?"

"What?"

"Coffee. Black or white?"

"Black? I think? I don't really drink it."

"Do you want tea instead?"

"Don't mind."

Paolo poured hot coffee and then brewed strong tea in one of the oversized mugs Toni's was famous for. He fetched milk from the fridge, added enough to make the tea rosy, and held the mug out.

Luis hesitated a moment before he took it. "I used to get these from your granddad back in the day."

"Which day?"

"Fridays, after school on my way to my, uh, brother's house."

"Oh. I didn't do Fridays. That was band practice at All Saints."

Luis's eyebrows shot up. "You went to All Saints?"

"Yup. I was in your year." Paolo nodded to the tables. "Shall we sit down?"

He rounded the counter without waiting for an answer and took a seat at the family table. Luis followed, brows drawn together in a deep, bemused frown.

Paolo eyed him. "What is it?"

"Nothing, I just . . ."

"What? Spit it out, mate."

Luis treated him to a faint smile. "I don't understand how we went to school together and I don't remember you."

"It's pretty simple. I was one of the guitar emos who hung out at the music block, and we had no classes together. Also, you were never there, and even when you were, I'm pretty sure you spent most of your time behind the tennis shed with Tanesha Johnson, so . . ."

It was Paolo's turn to trail off as Luis's smile sharpened to the kind of smirk Paolo had expected from him all along. But it didn't reach his eyes, and it was gone before it truly solidified, leaving in place the frown that aged his lovely face by a decade he didn't deserve. "Still feels weird that I don't remember you."

"Why?"

Luis tapped his fingers on the table. Opened his mouth. Shut it again. "Doesn't matter. What do you want to talk about?"

For the life of him, Paolo couldn't remember. Abruptly, he was sixteen again and casting furtive glances across the corridor at the popular boys who smelt of hair gel and cigarette smoke. He couldn't recall most of their faces now, but he remembered Luis, with his gold rings and mean stare, and yet somehow the sweetest smile that had driven all the girls wild—

Luis's drumming fingers got louder. Paolo blinked and forced himself back into the present. "So . . . we need to talk about money and hours. I work all day every day, but I don't expect you to do that."

"I can if you want. Haven't got anything better to do."

As tempting as it was to have full-time help, Paolo's conscience wouldn't allow him to inflict his punishing schedule on anyone else. "I can give you six days, Monday to Saturday? Six till three? It's £10.75 an hour, which I know isn't—"

"How much?"

Paolo repeated the figure. "I know it's shit, but it's LLW, and—"

"LL what?"

"The London Living Wage. You know, the—oh fuck. I don't suppose you do. It's pretty new."

"Is it the same as minimum wage?"

"No. It's higher, and not legally binding. I can pay you £8.20 if you'd prefer?"

"Is that minimum wage? Jesus. I thought it was six quid or some shit. Even £8.20 would make me fucking rich."

Luis's relieved grin was gorgeous.

And infectious.

Paolo smiled too. "Seriously? I figured whatever I paid you would be peanuts compared to whatever you did for money before you went down. I've seen your boys in their flash cars."

Luis's good humour faded. "They're not my boys."

"What about your brother?"

"What about him? I already told you I don't run with Moss Farm anymore."

He had. More than once. And given his joy at an extra few quid an hour, Paolo was starting to believe him. "Anyway, you won't pay much tax on that as most of it will come under your annual allowance, so you'll probably end up with about twelve hundred a month. Can you live on that?"

"I guess so. After rent and bills, I haven't got anything to spend it on."

"What about going out? Clothes and stuff?"

Luis laughed, but it was devoid of humour and did nothing to light up his face. "Yeah. Next question."

Paolo hadn't intended on asking him anything aside from his preference for working hours, but the longer they talked, the more he wanted to. Luis fascinated him for all kinds of reasons, none of them good. "How do you want to be paid? Weekly? Monthly? I can pay cash if you want, but it still has to go through the books."

"I wouldn't want it off the books. I need a real job to keep my place. But it might take me a while to figure my bank account stuff out. I don't know any of the details, and I lost all my ID before I went away, so I can't open a new one."

"Did you call them?"

"Who?"

"The bank."

"No."

"Maybe go down there? Do you have a letter from your landlord and your prison paperwork? That might be enough."

Luis shrugged, and Paolo thought hard for a solution that wouldn't see him starve. "How are you paying your rent?"

"With a payment card at the post office."

"So you can pay that with cash?"

"I think so."

"Okay, well, find out. If you can, I'll pay you in cash until you have your accounts up and running. If not, I'll hold your rent money and come with you to pay it by card."

"Why would you do that?"

Paolo had no idea. He offered a shrug of his own. "You're no good to me if you're homeless."

Luis nodded. "Fair enough."

It really wasn't, but they'd run out of time to talk about it. Paolo drained his coffee mug and got up to refill it for the first of the many he'd need to get through the day. He turned to offer Luis more tea, but he was already in the kitchen, rummaging in the fridge for tomatoes and mushrooms.

He found the green and brown chopping boards without being asked and got to work. Paolo figured it would keep him busy for a little while. He fired up the grill and stacked the bread by the toaster. Two fresh mugs of coffee found their way into his belly, but their effects were dampened by the bone-deep exhaustion hanging over him.

Just before six, his phone rang. It was Toni.

"What happened?"

Paolo swallowed a sigh. "She fell in the bathroom. They thought she'd broken her hip, but it's just a bruise. She's okay now."

Toni cursed in Italian and set off on a rant that made Paolo's ears bleed and his heart ache. His grandparents landing in separate care homes had been the worst thing that had ever happened, and guilt burned craters in his soul that the cafe didn't make enough money to put it right. Hell, it barely made enough to cover the fractional amount he paid to Toni's home each month.

With Toni still talking, Paolo set the egg pans to heat, drifted to the front door, and unlocked it on autopilot. A handful of waiting tradesmen wandered in; some faces Paolo knew, others he didn't.

The ones he knew nodded in greeting. Paolo nodded

back and gestured to his phone. "Be with you in a sec," he mouthed. And to Toni, "Nonno, I've got to go. It's opening time. I'll call you later, okay?"

Toni sighed with the weight of the world. "Okay, but don't come and see me tonight. I want you to go and be with Nonna, even if they'll only let you in for a little while. It frightens me so much to think of her alone."

"She's not alone. She's got friends there, and I'll take you to see her on Sunday."

After sixty years of marriage, it was a sad offering, but it was all Paolo had, and Toni knew it. He bid Paolo goodbye and hung up, leaving Paolo to face the world alone.

5

Luis worked as he'd done the day before, a machine of silence and efficiency. From time to time, Paolo found himself watching him, tracking his every move and the expressions on his lovely face as he made them.

He was cute as hell when he was concentrating, all frowns and dimples. Quiet, though. Too quiet. He spoke to no one, not even Paolo, unless Paolo asked him a direct question, and even that was a stretch. Half of Paolo's efforts to communicate went unanswered, and after a while, he stopped bothering. Another day he might've persisted, but fatigue erased his patience.

Not that he'd had much to begin with, especially on a day like today when his existence seemed wired to annoy him. The gas grill's flickering pilot light, the leaking milk container, and the dripping tap in the kitchen. By the time a full basket of bread slipped out of Paolo's hand, he was done.

Sliced loaves covered the floor. Paolo swore loud

enough for every table in the cafe to pause and stare, and it took every ounce of self-restraint not to hurl the empty basket at them.

He dropped to the floor to clean up the mess.

Luis was already there. He gathered the loaves in ten seconds flat, loaded them into the basket and wordlessly handed it over.

Paolo took it and straightened up, but by the time he got there, Luis had already vanished back into the kitchen. Paolo's gaze flickered between the open door and the full breadbasket in his hand. *Did that even happen?*

Without the still-staring customers, he might've believed it hadn't.

Confused, he took the bread to the grill and finished up the orders lined up on the pass. The breakfast rush was starting to fade. He delivered the final plates of fried eggs, black pudding, and grilled tomatoes, and returned to the grill to take a breather. He cleaned down with shaky hands. The half dozen mugs of coffee in his belly were threatening to mutiny, and he needed to eat.

More bacon found its way to the grill. For him alone, he might've left it at that. Slapped it between two slices of buttered bread and called it a day. But Luis hadn't eaten either, and after the splatted eggs of the previous day, Paolo felt like he owed him a decent plate of food.

He added sausages to the grill, the slim, Italian kind that were chilli hot and cooked fast. More eggs. One day he'd sit down and try and count how many he'd fried in his lifetime, but today wasn't that day. He made toast, topped it with leftover tomatoes, and carried the loaded plates to the family table.

Then he braced himself and stepped into the kitchen.

Luis was at the sink, face creased into that damn adorable frown, piecing the broken tap back together with tools Paolo hadn't known existed. He didn't seem to notice Paolo in the doorway. He screwed the final part on and twisted the tap to life. Water gushed into the sink. Luis nodded to himself and turned it off again.

No drip.

For the first time in months, *no fucking drip.* Paolo started forward, checked himself, and changed direction so Luis saw him coming. "You fixed it."

A tiny smile danced across Luis's full lips. "I tried. I wasn't sure it would work."

"Well, thank you. That piece of shit has been broken for months. Actually, maybe years. It all blurs together after a while."

"I know." Luis wiped his hands. "Um, I don't want to be a ball ache, but do you have a spare apron anywhere I could use? Wet jeans do my head in."

"Didn't I give you one?"

"I don't think so."

"Damn. Sorry. I've got one at home for you, but I forgot to bring it. Last night was a thing. Can you get by today?"

Luis nodded. "I can get by forever. I just wondered if you had one lying around."

"You don't have to get by forever. I'll sort it for you."

"Okay."

Luis turned back to the sink and Paolo to the kitchen

GARRETT LEIGH

door. Then he remembered why he'd sought Luis out in the first place. "Hey, I've got some breakfast for you out front if you want it?"

No reply.

Paolo frowned. It made sense that Luis would ignore him when he was busy at the dishwasher or if whatever Paolo had said didn't require a response, but their conversation had ended recently enough that even Luis hadn't had time to check out. He tried again. "Luis. You want breakfast, mate?"

Still nothing. Cautious, Paolo stepped back into the space he'd occupied a moment ago and waved his hands.

Luis looked up. "Yeah?"

Paolo pointed out front. "I made breakfast. Come find me when you're ready."

He left Luis to the sink and tracked back out front to wait for him, mind whirring. For days, he'd assumed Luis's silence was deliberate. Never once had he considered the possibility that Luis couldn't—

"Wow. Thanks. What's on the tomatoes?"

"Oregano." Paolo watched—*ogled*—as Luis slid into his seat, folding his long legs beneath the table. Their knees were a hairsbreadth apart, and Paolo's skin tingled, nerve ends jangling. *God, this is insane.* "Toni was always trying to sneak *Italiano* into the fry-ups that paid the bills."

"What about these?" Luis pointed to the sausages.

"Yeah. Those too. They're pretty poky, though. Sorry, I should've asked you if you liked spicy things."

"I think so. It's been a while. Inside, the closest thing to flavour is the Pot Noodles you buy from the canteen."

"How does that work?"

"Pot Noodles?"

"No, buying things. You can work for extra money, right? Did you have a job?"

Luis picked up a fork. "That's a lot of questions."

"Sorry. You don't have to answer."

"It's okay. They warn you before you come out that random people will ask weird questions. I don't mind."

Random people? Paolo couldn't imagine anyone approaching Luis in the street. *Or does he mean me?* Either way, the phrase sat awkwardly in the place Luis had carved out for himself in Paolo's tired mind. *Food. I need food. Maybe then I'll stop being a weirdo.* He gestured for Luis to start eating and dug into his own plateful, clearing half of it before he looked up again.

Luis's plate was empty. *Shit. Did I not give him enough?* Or maybe that was how they ate in prison, quick-sharp, before someone else took it. Or maybe—

Fuck's sake. Stop ruminating over shit you know nothing about.

Paolo finished his breakfast and got up to fetch tea and coffee. When he got back, Luis was leaning back in his chair, legs stretched out, head tipped back. His eyes were closed. Paolo placed two steaming mugs on the table and nudged his foot. "Tea's up."

Luis roused himself. "Thanks. Didn't hear you coming."

"That happen often?"

"What? That you sneak up on me? It's only been two days, mate."

"That's not what I meant."

Luis sipped his tea and shot Paolo a quizzical glance over his mug. The rational human fighting for survival in Paolo screamed at him to mind his own business, but the nosy old woman in him couldn't stop. "You don't hear me a lot. Probably not a bad thing most of the time when I'm shouting about burnt toast and the football, but I'm wondering if there's something I need to know."

"Like what?"

"Like, if you have an issue I should be helping you more with. Or if it's something that puts you at risk in a busy kitchen. Like, what if the gas alarm went off and you didn't hear it?"

"I'd smell it."

"What about the fire alarm?"

"I'd smell the fire too."

"You're missing the point."

"I'm really not." Luis set his mug down. "You're asking me stuff that doesn't give you the answer you want."

There was no challenge in Luis's tone, only truth. Paolo leaned forwards, seeking more. "I think you're struggling to hear out of your left ear. Am I right?"

"Yeah."

"Why?"

"Because you're smart enough to figure it out, I guess."

"That's not what I—"

"I know." Another of Luis's ghost-like smiles warmed his face. "I'm being a dick, sorry."

"Don't be. I don't mind."

"You didn't give me that impression when I first got here."

"There's different levels of dick."

Luis met Paolo's gaze head on, his golden eyes steady. "That right?"

Paolo swallowed, hiding his face behind his coffee mug. Anyone else, he might've thought they were flirting, but . . . not Luis Pope. He was taking the piss. He had to be, because the alternative was mind-blowing.

And flattering. When was the last time a bloke as hot as him looked your way twice?

Too long ago to remember, but then, Paolo's love life was time constrained to the occasional Scruff hook-up, so . . .

"Anyway." Paolo cleared his throat. "Am I right about your hearing?"

Luis gazed at him for another drawn-out moment, then nodded with a heavy sigh. "You're right. I got by with it for a while, but it's getting worse."

"What's caused it?"

"You really want to know?"

"Asked, didn't I?"

"Yeah, but you said you didn't want any road shit up in your face."

"I meant that in the literal sense, not that you had to pretend you're someone else."

Luis's eyebrows twitched.

Paolo snorted. "Okay, maybe I did mean that. But whatever. I'm an arsehole. I say and mean lots of things in the heat of the moment."

"Like what?"

Like stuff you're too straight to ever hear. "Stop evading. It'll be lunchtime at this rate."

Beaten, or perhaps bored of their dance, Luis leaned forwards too. Both hunched over the table, Lord knew what they looked like to anyone watching, but Paolo didn't care, and maybe, just maybe, neither did Luis.

He raised his hand. For a heart-stopping second, Paolo thought he might touch his face. But he didn't. He pushed his own hair back, revealing an ugly, ragged scar on his scalp. "Retaliation," he said. "For something Dante had fucked up on the outside. Someone had to pay, and apparently, I hadn't paid enough for his bullshit."

Paolo's fingers itched to trace the scar. It was clearly old, but the vicious line of raised flesh turned his stomach. "What happened?"

"Got jumped in the showers and whacked with a pipe. Knocked me out for two days and damaged the auditory nerve in my brain."

"How bad?"

"I don't know. I got away with it for a while, but it's got worse in the last year."

"Can they do anything to fix it?"

"Dunno."

Paolo eyed Luis and set his mug down. Was his vague answer another deflection, or did he really not know? His expression was as open as Paolo had ever seen it, but after two short days with the man, what did he know?

In any case, the cafe had begun to fill up again, and it was time to get back to work.

The lunch rush came and went. With Luis clearing the tables, Paolo's tired self felt like he was on holiday. Perversely, the lack of absolute chaos kicked his fatigue up a gear. He made mistakes. Got mad. Repeated them.

"I asked for beans, mate. Not tomatoes."

Paolo glared at the hipster with the ludicrous facial hair. *Is that a thing now? Porn-star moustaches?* Maybe he needed to get out more.

Or not, if it meant waxing handlebars. "We don't do beans."

"Why didn't you tell me that when I ordered then? I don't like tomatoes."

"Like I give a shit." Paolo snatched the plate back and stomped into the kitchen. He tossed it into the sink, food and all.

It broke.

Luis appeared from the back door, a roll of fresh bin bags tucked under his arm. He glanced between Paolo and the sink. "They didn't like it?"

"I didn't like *him*. He's a prick with turd-coloured pipe cleaners stuck to his face."

"So . . . what are you going to do? Punch him?"

"What? No. I wish."

"I can tell. And so will he if you go back out there looking like that."

"Yeah, well. He's not a regular so I don't give a fuck."

"Uh-huh." Luis reached into the sink and retrieved the fragmented plate. He disappeared with it, leaving Paolo to seethe in peace and stare at the mess of food in the sink. *Clean it up.* But he didn't have time. Hipster Prick needed his order, and Paolo needed to deliver it without lamping him in the face.

Still grumbling, he returned to the grill and plated up a fresh lunch. He took it out, but the man with the bad moustache had gone, having opened every packet of sugar in the bowl and emptied them on the table.

Rage swept through Paolo. He'd never been good at hiding his feelings, and right now, he didn't care who knew it. He dropped the plate of food on the table and burst out of the front door. Hipster man was twenty feet up the road, loping along in his tweed trousers. *Fucking dick*. Paolo started forwards but strong arms hauled him back.

"Don't," Luis said. "His dad's a copper."

His lips were close to Paolo's ear, so close his warm breath sent shivers down Paolo's spine, but his temper was hot and strong, and for a moment he fought the glorious arms wrapped tight around him. "So? What's he gonna do? Arrest me for telling his kid he's an arsehole?"

"I've been nicked for less."

Paolo grunted, but though his temper burned bright, it had the stamina of a pound-shop firework.

It fizzled out.

He stopped struggling, and Luis let him go.

Bemused, Paolo spun around. Luis stood behind him, expression so hard to read it was as if he didn't have one. "That bloke was a prick."

Luis nodded. "I know."

"You should've let me deck him."

"Why? He'd still win. You'd just be the immigrant yob who'd put him in hospital."

Paolo scoffed. "I wouldn't have hit him that hard."

"Yeah, but did you see him? One fucking flick and he'd have a concussion and compensation claim."

Luis was right, obviously. But Paolo still wanted to kill someone, because it was that or contemplate how crazy-hot Luis's arms had felt around him. Sure and strong and yet so thrilling it was hard to believe Luis had let him go yet. The rollercoaster was still running, twisting and turning, spinning every thought that passed through his head upside down.

Man, I wish he hadn't done that. Not because thumping a hipster was his lifelong ambition. Nah, but because now it didn't matter how the rest of the day played out, not a minute would go by when he didn't think about those damn fucking arms.

6

Paolo was a book Luis couldn't put down. One minute he was cooking lunch for the five thousand and whistling along with the radio, the next he was charging down the street, ready to kill over a plate of tomatoes.

It would've been funny if he wasn't so god damn hot.

And he was friendlier than his regular outbursts belied. For two weeks straight, except Sundays, he made Luis breakfast and sent him home with a foil-wrapped parcel for dinner. Luis wondered if he'd get sick of eggs and bacon, but it had been the best part of a week, and he wasn't there yet.

Or maybe it wasn't the bacon he couldn't get enough of. Maybe it was the random conversations that tricked Luis into spilling his guts about stuff he hadn't talked about in years, at least not to anyone who wasn't paid to pretend they cared. Because it had to be a trick. Luis had a gold medal in keeping his shit to himself. He didn't blab to strangers. Or even his friends, not that he had many of those in his camp anymore.

Fucking witchcraft. Has to be.

Sunday was Luis's day off, but after kicking around the bedsit all morning and driving himself crazy, he showed up at the cafe anyway.

Paolo met him at the back door. "Did you forget something?"

Luis debated bullshitting him but shook his head. "You said you do different food on Sundays. Thought I'd have a look in case you ever, uh, need me." *Twat. You do the dishes. What difference does it make what's on them?*

None that he could think of, but if Paolo thought it strange that he'd rocked up at work for fun, it didn't show, and Paolo Cilberto was a man who wore his every thought and emotion on his sleeve.

That was how Luis knew he had family shit going on that was keeping him up at night. That every time his phone rang, it was someone who said things that broke his heart. *No, you know that because you spend all day gawping at him and accidentally-ish listening in on his phone calls.*

Whatever. The details weren't important. Paolo waved Luis inside like it made perfect sense, and that was enough for Luis. He followed Paolo through the kitchen and out to the front of the cafe. In place of the stacks of sizzling bacon, vats of baked pasta sat on the counter, kept warm on hot plates. Bowls of salad filled the refrigerated display, and loaves of Italian bread were stacked where the sliced white usually sat.

It smelt amazing. And Paolo was different too. The

frenetic energy that seemed to carry him through the weekday chaos was absent. He leaned on the counter, a picture of relaxation and a far cry from the maniac who just last week had wanted to murder a hipster. *Damn. Could he get any more gorgeous?*

Paolo smiled. Apparently, he could. "So . . ." He gestured at the pasta trays. "There's not much to what we do on Sundays. Make some sauce, cook some pasta, mix it all together, and serve it to whoever wanders in."

"You make it sound so simple."

"It is compared to a hundred million fry-ups. It's a piece of piss, and we don't get that busy. Toni only started opening on Sunday's for his mates. They're all dead now, though, so why I'm still bothering, I have no fucking clue."

"Nostalgia?"

"More like I have nothing else to do, and we need the money, as little as it is."

"Know that feeling, on both counts."

Paolo gave Luis one of those looks that flayed him wide open. The kind of look that had led to Luis giving a voice to the past. The scar on his head came to life, tingling like it was brand new, not years old. Luis forced himself not to touch it and thrust his hands in his pockets. "Anyway, I better get going, unless you need any help?"

"I don't, but stick around if you want. I might put the football on in a bit."

Luis couldn't have cared less about the beautiful game, but Paolo's offer was too tempting to refuse. Waking up with nothing to do had done his head in. He'd bought bread the day before, some tins of beans, butter, teabags, and milk, but his solitary breakfast had tasted like card-board, and the silence had got under his skin. Pacing the bedsit hadn't panned out, and so here he was, loitering like a loser.

But as Paolo smiled at him and handed him a mug of magical tea, he couldn't bring himself to regret it. He took a deep sip and glanced through the open kitchen door at the dishwasher. A few loads were stacked up. It wasn't much, but still.

He stepped towards it.

Paolo stopped him, wrapping long, elegant fingers around his elbow. "Don't you dare. It's your day off."

"I don't mind."

"I do. I need you firing on all cylinders tomorrow, not whacked out cos you haven't had a proper day off."

Luis snorted. "It won't kill me to clear the decks. Besides, what about *your* day off?"

"Not your concern."

It wasn't, but despite Paolo's chill demeanour, it was obvious he was knackered. His olive complexion was paler than usual, and dark circles smudged the skin beneath his eyes. Fighting him, though, would bring nothing but trouble. Obeying his order was the easy option, but nothing in Luis's life had ever been easy.

He covered Paolo's hand with his own and slowly—reluctantly—peeled his fingers away. "It's not my concern, but the dishwasher will be tomorrow. Don't want to spend all day cleaning up your mess."

"Very funny—"

"What? Can't hear you. Sorry."

Luis stepped out of Paolo's grasp and slipped into the kitchen, bracing himself for Paolo to follow and rip him a new one. But it didn't happen. He made it to the dishwasher unmolested—*shame*—and mowed through the loads stacked up in the sink.

With that done, he braved a peek through the kitchen door. Paolo was serving at the counter. Luis took his chance and slipped out to clear a table, and the dance continued all day long until Paolo shut the cafe at two.

He came to find Luis in the kitchen, a bottle of Italian beer in each hand. He handed one to Luis. "Now it's my day off. Come and eat."

Luis wasn't about to argue with that. His lonely breakfast seemed a lifetime ago. He took the proffered beer and followed Paolo out front. The vats of baked pasta still held enough for twenty people, though Luis reckoned he was hungry enough to put a serious dent in it.

Paolo passed him a plate. "Fill your boots, mate. Any leftovers go to the night shelter at the Methodist church, but they only take ten in every night, so they won't need all this."

"You sure?"

"Wouldn't say it if I wasn't."

Fair enough. Luis took the plate and piled it high with penne pasta baked with meat sauce and cheese. "This shit is like spag bol on steroids."

Paolo laughed. "Don't say that in front of anyone from my family. My nonna would give you a clip round the ear if she could reach that high."

He filled his own plate and pointed at the table Luis had come to think of as theirs. "Sit."

Luis sat and dug into his food. It was delicious and so different from the all-day breakfasts he'd grown used to in the last week, he cleared his plate in two minutes flat.

Paolo ate slower, sipping his beer. "Anyone would think I didn't feed you."

"You don't have to, you know. You never said free food came with the job."

"It's not free. You work for it."

"That's a generous way of looking at it. I don't reckon they get a free lunch at Tesco."

"You don't work at Tesco."

Paolo was good at these conversations, at firing back statements that proved nothing except the fact that he possessed a razor-sharp tongue. Luis recognised them as armour for a man unable to accept he was doing a nice thing, and that, more than anything, made Paolo unlike anyone he'd ever known.

Luis drank his beer while Paolo finished his food. The boozy bubbles slipped down like a dream and fizzed in his belly. He drained the bottle and held it up to the light. "I've never had this brand before. It's good."

Paolo grinned a little. "I'd get you another, but I drank them all last Sunday. I've got some of Toni's old plonk out the back, though. Hang on."

"It's okay—"

But Paolo was already on his feet and walking away. He came back with a dusty bottle and two glasses. "Don't worry. It tastes better than it looks."

He poured dark red wine into the glasses and slid one across the table to Luis.

Luis picked it up and swirled it around. "I've never drunk this before either. Is it strong? I can't remember the last time I had a drink."

Lies. The last drink Luis had taken had been a shot of cheap vodka in the back of a stolen car before the cluster-fuck of a job that had cost him six years of his life. The car had gone up in flames minutes later, glowing at the side of the road like a beacon of his sins. He could still smell the burnt rubber of the tyres.

Maybe the wine would help.

He took a tiny sip, and then a deeper one, as the round, fruity flavour coated his tongue and seared a path down his throat. "Wow. That's something else."

Paolo claimed his own glass and downed half the contents in a long swallow that worked his throat enough to send Luis back for another swig. "It's not bad. I'm not allowed to take it to Toni anymore, though. So looks like I'll have to drink it all myself."

"Why can't Toni have it?"

"House rules. He's in a care home now, and apparently they haven't got time to deal with inebriated geriatrics."

"What about your grandma?"

"Nonna? She's in a different place. A nursing home." Paolo reached for the bottle. "She's not allowed any fun either, but I reckon I want to talk about that as much as you do your brother, so let's move on, eh?"

Luis didn't need telling twice. He let Paolo refill his glass and drank more wine, enjoying the cocoon of warmth that settled around him. Around them. Locked up in the cafe, it felt like they were the only souls left in the world, and he was okay with that.

More than okay. Paolo checked in with the football results, and Luis let his mind drift. A week ago, he'd been preparing for release, ready to leave prison behind, and yet terrified of the blank space in front of him. Then he'd been running scared from the job centre one day and pleading with the teenage girl behind the counter in the bank to unlock his account, despite his lack of photo ID. Working for Paolo had filled the gaps enough to calm him, but a sense of impending doom still haunted him. Holed up in the cafe with a full belly, booze, and a beautiful man for company was too good to be true.

It had to be.

Paolo nudged Luis's arm, fingers trailing over his fore-arm ... Or were they? Maybe it was all in Luis's head. And if it was, who cared? There were worse things to fantasise about.

The bottle of wine grew empty. Paolo made small talk. Luis responded with words, none of them important. The wine settled in his blood, warming his soul. He felt tired but too content to fall asleep and miss a moment.

He felt like someone else.

Paolo nudged him again—Luis had no clue how long it had been since the first time. "We've run out of booze. Probably time to call it a night."

Luis couldn't think of anything he wanted to do less than walk home in the cold to his barren bedsit, but that wasn't Paolo's concern. He shrugged and got to his feet. "Do you want me to help lock up?"

"If you want."

It was as good an offer as any. Luis set the chairs on the table while Paolo locked the back door and mopped the floors.

They met at the front door and stepped out into the night. "I live in the flats behind the petrol station," Paolo said. "That's on your way, right?"

Luis nodded.

"Come on, then." Paolo set off, and Luis followed, falling into step beside him. It was strange to see Paolo outside of the cafe. The city was the same as it had always been, but its monotony didn't suit Paolo's beauty. It was like watching a puma prowl through the supermarket, dangerous and ethereal and not quite right.

"You're so quiet," Paolo remarked. "It freaked me out at first, but I like it now. It's so different from how my family used to be."

"Your grandparents?"

"Yeah. They were like the quintessential Italian couple, always yelling at each other, Toni ducking from all the shit my nonna threw at him."

"What about your parents?"

"Didn't really have any. Smackheads, the both of them. Long dead now. What about yours?"

"My mum lives in Birmingham. We don't speak. And I never knew my dad."

"Why don't you speak to your mum?"

Luis shrugged. "She's not very nice."

"That's as good a reason as any."

"I know, right? Dante—uh, my brother used to keep in touch with her. He paid for her boob job."

Paolo whistled. "Your family sound as fucked up as mine."

"They are, but I don't see them as my family anymore. I'm not the same person I was before, and I don't care about them."

"I know how that goes. For a long time, I was angry with my parents for being useless shits, then one day I grew up and stopped giving a fuck. Stopped missing a life I'd never had, you know?"

"I know."

Paolo trailed to a stop. Luis glanced up and realised they were in front of the blocks of flats that hadn't existed before he'd gone inside. Clean white cladding and a thousand windows, they looked like the new prison wing he'd watched go up during his last two years, but he kept that thought to himself. "This is you?"

"Yup." Paolo fished in his pocket for a set of keys. "How long does it take you to get home?"

"Fifteen minutes. It's not that far."

"Far enough, though, eh? Seeing as you still don't own a coat."

"How do you know I don't own one? Maybe I'm just hardy."

"Viking, are you?"

"Maybe." Luis started to back up, to turn around and disappear into the night.

Paolo's hand shot out to stop him. "Fuck this cold, mate. Do you want to come in?"

————

Paolo's flat smelt like the cafe had that day, of herbs and contentment. Luis shut the door behind him and leaned against it a moment, breathing it all in. "Did you cook the pasta here?"

"I did, actually. How can you tell?"

"I can smell it."

"Good. My neighbour hates garlic and he's a right dickhead, so I do what I can to annoy him."

"That bad?"

"He called the police on the little old lady below me because she had pot plants outside her front door. The bloke's a psycho."

"Sounds it."

Paolo grunted and slid his coat from his fine shoulders and then peeled off his T-shirt, swapping it for another that was draped over the arm of the couch.

Luis tried not to stare. Paolo was narrower than him, but his sinewy muscle screamed strength in a way that made Luis feel hot all over. Or maybe it was the wine. He hadn't been drunk in forever, and he'd forgotten how much he liked it. How, if he balanced it right and didn't neck too much, the sweet oblivion was gentle enough to carry him away from the world for a while. The real world, at least. Not the one where he was nosing around Paolo's flat while Paolo took his clothes off. That world could stick around as long as it liked.

Paolo's flat was a tidy bachelor pad, equipped with a big TV, games consoles, and just the right amount of mess to let Luis know that no girlfriend shared the space. *What if he's got a boyfriend, though?*

Luis couldn't decide how he felt about that. On the one hand, it made more sense than someone as hot as Paolo being single. On the other, it made the daft notion that Paolo was flirting with him nearly real.

Nearly.

Paolo fetched beer from his tiny kitchen and directed Luis to the sofa in his open plan living room. After the warming red wine, the cold bubbles woke Luis up. He drank slowly, eyeing Paolo over his bottle, trying not to notice his full lips, elegant neck, or how his throat worked as he swallowed. But it was tough. And he failed. He shifted on the couch, wishing he'd worn jeans. More small talk flowed between them. Paolo, it seemed, could talk shit for hours, and Luis didn't mind. Away from the stress of the busy cafe, Paolo was calm, and he smiled a lot. It was a far cry from the crazy person he'd been the day before, and Luis was enchanted. He stayed as long as decency allowed, but eventually, the beer ran out, and Paolo stopped talking.

Luis rose from the couch. "I'd better go."

Paolo said nothing and trailed him to the front door, leaning on the wall as Luis stepped into his shoes. "You have nice shaped feet."

"Er, thanks? I think?"

A slow laugh dripped from Paolo, giving away the beer and wine they'd shared. "You're welcome. I didn't mean it in a weirdo way."

"I didn't take it in a weirdo way."

"Good."

"Yeah. Good." Luis straightened. Paolo hadn't moved but somehow seemed closer in the dimly lit hallway. His body heat thrummed in Luis's blood, and Luis's heart seemed to beat in time with the pulse in Paolo's neck. Luis stepped closer, and Paolo pushed off the wall. They met in the middle. Luis snatched a breath, and then madness overcame him. He put his palms flat on Paolo's chest, pushed him against the front door, and kissed him.

A distant horror fought for dominance with the wild sensation that swept over him, but Paolo kissed him back with zero hesitation, eviscerating any fear that Luis had made a terrible mistake. He flattened himself against the door, drawing Luis closer. His tongue slipped between Luis's lips with the sweetest groan, and Luis knew without a shadow of drunken doubt, the earth could erupt beneath them and their mouths would stay fused together.

I could kiss him forever.

7

Paolo paced the cafe with scratchy eyes and an aching head, listening out for the tap at the back door, despite the fact that it was, as ever, four in the morning, a full hour before Luis usually showed up for work. And even that was another hour before his official start time. There was every chance he wouldn't rock up until six. *If he turns up at all.*

Groaning, Paolo dropped into the nearest chair and buried his head in his hands. His memories of last night were fuzzy thanks to the bottle of Toni's finest they'd sunk. He should've warned Luis that shit crept up on a man, but he'd been too busy kissing him. *Idiot. He's supposed to be able to trust you, not worry about you throwing yourself at him every time you have a beer together.*

Reason told Paolo it hadn't gone down that way. That it was Luis who'd made the first move. Luis who'd pushed him against the front door and kissed him. Luis who made his dick so hard it gave him a stomach ache. But as Paolo sat alone in the dark cafe, reason seemed a distant memory. All he could clearly recall was waking alone on the couch with the imprint of Luis's mouth on his lips.

Damn fucking chianti.

With another groan, he hauled himself to his feet and finished up the jobs he'd neglected last night. At quarter to five, the delivery arrived with crates of bacon, sausages, eggs, and black pudding. The bakery lorry arrived next with the bread. And then the milkman, and the green-grocer with the mushrooms and tomatoes. Paolo signed for it all, then gazed around the kitchen. Putting the deliveries away by himself had been his normal until a few weeks ago, but he'd grown used to Luis helping, or sometimes even taking the task away from Paolo entirely. *How did I ever manage without him?*

The thought solidified the fear that he'd truly fucked up last night. If Luis freaked out and left, Paolo would be on his own again, and it scared him more than he cared to admit. Less work gave him more time to do the things that mattered, like keeping the accounts in order and visiting Toni and Nonna. Like sleeping and eating proper meals. Luis's company mattered too. He didn't talk much, but he didn't have to. His quiet presence was a balm to Paolo's noisy soul, and Paolo needed that in his life like he needed cold beer and hot coffee. More than that.

Despite waiting for the soft tap at the back door, when it came, Paolo jumped a mile. He set down the box of bacon he'd been ferrying to the fridge and opened the door.

Luis was stood where he usually stood, three feet back,

as if he expected the door to be slammed in his face, half hidden by the shadows of the lingering night. A night that had ended with them kissing against a different door.

Stop it.

Paolo waved Luis inside. Luis passed him in a haze of fresh scented shampoo and man, and Paolo's head spun, but he blamed the smouldering hangover at the base of his skull and ignored it. "Can you put the rest of this away? I need to brush down the grill."

Luis nodded. "Sure."

He reached for the bacon box Paolo had abandoned and took it to the fridge. Despite having a million and one things to do, Paolo didn't move.

Luis came back and eyed him over the stack of boxes still cluttering the kitchen. "What's up?"

"What?"

"You seem out of it. Hungover?"

"Little bit," Paolo admitted. "What about you?"

"Not yet. Ask me at lunchtime."

Luis's grin was as quiet as the rest of him, and Paolo spent much of their time together chasing it down, needling Luis until he set it free, but in the growing light of the early morning, it wasn't enough. Paolo was torn between wanting to punch him and kissing him again.

And again. And again.

He couldn't remember why they'd stopped.

Lacking any brighter ideas, he decamped to the coffee machine and added an extra scoop of ground beans to a brew that was already rocket fuel. He made Luis a mug of tea and took it back into the kitchen. Luis was in the fridge, and lingering made Paolo feel like a creep.

He dumped it on the side and fled.

The morning slipped away, lost to the daily grind of prepping the cafe for the day and then opening the doors. Breakfast came and went. Luis bussed tables and ran the dishwasher with the silence and efficiency he always did, and it was as if nothing had happened. As if nothing had changed between them, and perhaps it hadn't. A drunken kiss proved nothing save the fact they were both queer as fuck and horny when they'd had a drink. Who knew? Maybe they'd fuck next time they shared a beer.

Or maybe they wouldn't. Maybe Luis would disappear after his shift like he'd done every day until yesterday and Paolo would never get to lay hands on him again. *Maybe—*

Paolo's phone rang, cutting off the irrational chain of maybes having a rave in his wine-pickled brain. Blinking, he pulled it from his back pocket, and his heart sank. It was Nonna's nursing home. *Shit.*

He abandoned the omelette he'd been making for him and Luis to share, slipped through the kitchen, and out of the back door. "Hello?"

"Hello, Paolo, it's Janine from Elm Lodge. I'm just calling to let you know your nonna's hip is giving her quite a lot of pain today. The doctor's been in and had a look at her, and he thinks it's best she pops into hospital to have another X-ray."

"Shit. How is she? Does she know what's going on?"

"A little, I think. I asked her if she was happy to go with

the paramedics when they arrive to fetch her, and she said yes."

Paolo sighed. "She'd say yes to anything these days. Probably thinks you're taking her to Brighton for fish and chips. How long is the transport going to be?"

"An hour or so. Would you like me to text you when it gets here? Or are you going to come in?"

"I'll come in, but I need to close the cafe and get on the bus, so could you let me know if it shows up so I can go straight to the hospital?"

Janine agreed and hung up, leaving Paolo to stare at his phone and contemplate closing the cafe before the lucrative lunchtime rush. The thrill in his gut faded. Suddenly, his late-night encounter with Luis seemed a long time ago.

He pocketed his phone and went back inside. Luis was still at the dishwasher, but he was leaning on it, arms folded, waiting for Paolo. "What's the matter?"

"I have to leave. My nonna's being taken to hospital."

"From the nursing home?"

"Yeah. She had a fall a week or so ago, and her hip isn't healing."

"Okay." Luis wiped his hands on the apron Paolo had finally got round to giving him. "Do you have any open orders?"

"No. There's some tables that have just sat down. I'll go tell them they have to go."

"Go? Why?"

"Because I have to close up." Paolo started for the kitchen door.

Luis grabbed his arm and pulled him back. "You don't have to close. I can cook until closing time."

"What?"

"I can cook and take the money if you trust me not to rob you blind."

"Why would you think that had even occurred to me?"

"Because you're looking at me funny."

"I—" Paolo shook his head to clear it. He felt like he was underwater. "Fuck, I really need to go."

"Then go. I got this, I promise."

Something clicked in Paolo's brain. He nodded slowly and untied his apron. Luis disappeared and came back with Paolo's coat and wallet. "Do you want me to lock up and go home or stay here until you get back?"

"Um, I don't know. I don't know how long I'll be."

"Want me to post the keys through your letterbox?"

"Yeah, actually, that would be great. Thank you."

"You're welcome. You want me to call you a taxi?"

"Nah, there's a bus in a couple of minutes." But Paolo didn't move. His feet were welded to the floor, his heart transfixed by the man in front of him. "Are you sure you'll be okay?"

Luis gripped Paolo's shoulders. For a moment, Paolo thought he might shake him, but he didn't. He wrapped his arms around Paolo and hugged him tight.

It felt like a lifetime had passed when he pulled back. "Go," he whispered. "I'll be here when you get back."

———

"Thanks, Janine."

Paolo shut the door on the heroic nurse and took a seat by Nonna's bed. She was sleeping now, like she did most of the day, apparently unaffected by her grand day out to the local A&E, and Paolo was glad of it. Nothing was worse than seeing his beloved grandmother in pain, and fuck knew, he'd seen it enough over the last few years.

He slumped in his chair. Now he knew Nonna was okay—for now—his brain kept trying to take him back to fretting about Luis and the cafe, but his worries found no traction. It was as if his heart knew something the rest of him didn't, and he couldn't make himself move. He woke Nonna up for dinner a little while later, helped her eat, and filmed her weekly message for Toni. Maybe at the weekend he'd bring Toni for a visit. Sunday, if he didn't spend it getting drunk and snogging Luis.

Like that's happening again.

Paolo's heart didn't believe that either.

The nurses arrived to give Nonna a bath. Paolo took his cue and left. On the bus home, he sent the video message to Toni and left out the part about the hospital trip. The X-rays hadn't revealed anything new.

He got off the bus at the wrong end of the high street. The walk back woke him up after the stuffy bus ride, and as he got closer to the cafe, he found himself jogging.

The front door was locked, but the lights were on.

It felt like a metaphor Paolo didn't quite understand. Then he saw Luis, sat at the family table, slumped over a newspaper, and nothing else seemed to matter. He rapped on the door. Luis didn't hear him. Paolo pulled out his phone and tapped out a message.

i'm here, let me in

Luis's phone flashed with the incoming message. He glanced at it and blurred across the cafe, moving faster than his tall frame should've allowed.

He unlocked the front door and pulled Paolo inside. "How is she? Is she okay?"

"She is now. They gave her an injection to help the inflammation." Paolo gazed around the cafe. It was spotless, cleaner than Paolo had ever left it in his entire life. The condiment bottles were full and wiped down, sugar packets topped up. Even the floor had been mopped and dried. "Wow. You went to town on this place. Was it that quiet?"

Luis shrugged. "The road was closed, remember? I left the order tickets by the till so you could match them up to the cash count. The card receipts are behind the twenties."

"Match them up? You think I pay that much attention?"

"Maybe, after you've left an ex-con in charge of your family business."

"Did you go to prison for stealing things?"

"Kind of."

Curiosity bubbled in Paolo's gut, but he swallowed it down. Toni had warned him against prying too deep into that part of Luis's story. *"Leave the past where it belongs, boy. Dragging it up won't help us trust him."*

Us. At the time, the word had infuriated Paolo. Where was the "us" when it was him who had to make the decision and bear the weight if he got it wrong? But Toni had been more right that he'd ever know. Paolo didn't care about Luis's mistakes. Fuck knows, he'd made plenty of his own.

He wandered to the till and opened the drawer. The cash levels looked the same as they always did after a weekday shift, especially one where traffic had been blocked off for most of it. He flipped through the card receipts and then the order slips Luis had clipped together in a neat stack. "Jesus. That's a lot of full fry-ups to cook by yourself. Are we gonna get rinsed on Trip Advisor?"

"Didn't have any complaints, so I hope not, mate."

Puzzled, Paolo slipped into the kitchen and inspected the fridge, the surgically clean dishwasher, and the dry store. He went back out front, studied the grill, and found it as clean as it had been when Uncle Romeo had installed it twenty years ago. *What am I missing?*

He spun around. While he'd run his inspection, Luis had gone back to his newspaper.

Paolo crossed the cafe and pulled out a chair dramatically enough to make Luis look up, though he didn't sit down. "All right. Spill. There's no way you ran that service by yourself with no training or experience. What gives?"

Luis sat back in his chair and folded his arms. "Nothing gives. I told you I could handle it, and I did. Did you want me to fuck it up?"

"No. I just had no idea you could run the cafe single-handed without me. Do you seriously think I'd have left you washing dishes all this time if I had?"

"I don't think you'd have ever left me alone regardless. You're a control freak, and I'm a convicted criminal."

77

Luis spoke with no inflection. Facts, not accusations.

Nothing Paolo could deny. "I'd never have left you because I didn't need to. But I wouldn't have kept you washing dishes and doing the shitty jobs all the time."

"I know."

"So why didn't you tell me?"

Luis started to shrug. Paolo growled and yanked him to his feet.

If Luis minded being manhandled, he hid it well. He let his folded arms drop and hang at his sides, expression bland.

Too bland.

Paolo let him go. "Sorry."

"Don't be. I like it when you put your hands on me."

"Do you?"

"Yes."

There was so much more Paolo needed to say. So much more he needed to ask, but as he stared at Luis and lost himself in every facet of his bewitching beauty, only one question blurted free. "Come home with me? Please?"

8

The walk home was like a dream. Fatigue pulled at Paolo's every sense, but Luis's presence beside him was a live wire of energy, keeping him moving.

He let them into his flat. Luis shut the door behind him and leaned against it, watching, as Paolo tossed his coat . . . somewhere and kicked off his shoes. "You did that yesterday. I thought it was because you were drunk, but you're just a messy sod."

"Yup. Fuck, was that only yesterday?"

"Yeah."

It was the first time they'd acknowledged it aloud, but it had smouldered between them all day until other things had taken over. And now it was back full force. Paolo's heart pounded, and heat sluiced through him. *I have to kiss him again.*

Paolo stepped into Luis's space. He palmed Luis's chest through his thin T-shirt and slid down to his flank. He tilted his head and eased himself between Luis's legs.

Their lips met, and just like the first time, the crackly connection between them exploded into something Paolo couldn't control. He crushed Luis into the door, kissing him over and over, tongues dancing, teeth clashing. Hard denim kept them apart, but Paolo felt *everything*, and the sensation of Luis's dick against his sent more jolts of crazy heat zipping around his body. *More, I need more.*

As if he'd spoken out loud, Luis drew back, breaking their kiss. His lips were redder than red, his gaze searching. "What do you want?"

Paolo shook his head, the ability to articulate the desire coursing through him long gone, if it had ever been there at all. He pulled Luis close again, spun him round, and backed him out of the hallway.

He didn't know where they were going. The bedroom felt presumptuous.

They wound up in the kitchen.

Luis swung them around again, and Paolo found himself against the counter as Luis tipped him backwards. *So much for control.* But Paolo didn't give a shit. Luis was every fantasy he'd ever had come true, and if he wanted to bend Paolo over the kitchen counter, Paolo wasn't going to stop him.

Couldn't stop him.

Luis slid his hands beneath Paolo's T-shirt, roaming Paolo's heated skin. He moved his lips to Paolo's neck like a god damn pro, and Paolo couldn't help the moan that burst free. *Too many clothes.* He tore his T-shirt over his head and reached for Luis's. The thin material disappeared, and in the dim light of the cramped kitchen, Luis's torso took Paolo's breath away. His skin was pale and flaw-less, punctuated by tattoos and a silver bar through one nipple.

Paolo wanted to tug it with his teeth.

He settled for another kiss. Skin touched skin, and it was Luis's turn to moan. He slid his hands over Paolo's hips, cupped the rounded muscle at the top of Paolo's legs, and in one fluid movement, hoisted Paolo onto the counter.

The position asserted the dominance Paolo was, uncharacteristically, happy to give up. It had been a long time since a man had last taken him apart the way Luis was, and he couldn't get enough.

Their kiss fell by the wayside. Luis undid Paolo's jeans, and Paolo wondered if he really was going to take him like that. Bend him over. Fuck him. His blood ran hot at the thought, but his heart told him that wasn't Luis's style. That he needed something else. They both did.

And perhaps Luis knew it too. He yanked Paolo's jeans down, his underwear too, and dropped his elbows on the counter. Paolo's cock sprang free, betraying—if he'd ever stood any chance of hiding it—how much he wanted this.

How much he wanted Luis.

And how fast his entire world had shifted on its axis. A month ago he'd been the loneliest queer in town. Now he was dropping his jeans for Luis Pope, and he had to wonder if he was legit having a fucked-up wet dream.

Yeah. That's right. For all the bad shit he'd heard about Luis and all the years he'd gone without seeing him, it had never stopped him picturing moments like this. Who wouldn't? Luis was stop-traffic gorgeous, and his mouth was inches away from Paolo's dick.

I've got to wake up soon. But nothing changed. Luis slid Paolo a shy smile, then he swooped, and nothing about the sensation that shot through Paolo was dreamlike. It was sharp, electrifying, and his answering groan was loud enough to rattle the walls.

"Fuck." His hands flew to Luis's shoulders. "Fuck, that's so hot."

Luis hummed, adding an extra layer of madness to the crazy pleasure his tongue and lips were already heaping on Paolo's cock.

It was insane. Hard, fast, and filthy, and Paolo couldn't take it. Pleasure ripped through him. He dug his fingers into Luis's shoulders, then tangled them in his silky hair. *God, his hair. I knew it would feel like this. So fucking soft.* But there was no time to appreciate it. Luis's mouth was doing the talking, and Paolo was in free fall. Ragged sounds fell from his lips. He steadied himself with one hand on the counter and twisted the fingers of the other deeper into Luis's hair. "If you're trying to make me come in ten seconds flat, you're going the right way about it."

Luis hummed again, but it was darker this time, and he tightened his grip on Paolo's hips, letting Paolo know he had no intention of easing off and every intention of making his gasped-out prophecy come true.

Paolo's mind blanked out, and he stopped caring about the complications that would inevitably come from messing around with his employee. From hooking up with Luis god damn Pope. Stopped caring about anything that wasn't his dick in Luis's mouth. Orgasm kicked its way through what little control he had left and tackled him to the ground. "Fuck, fuck, fuck, I'm gonna come."

He let go of Luis's hair, giving him room to pull away if he wanted to.

Luis didn't pull away. He took Paolo impossibly deeper. Paolo's cock scraped along the back of Luis's throat, and Paolo was done. Breath left his lungs. His hips flexed. Pent up desire spurted out of him and into Luis's waiting mouth. He shuddered, chest heaving. "Damn. Fucking damn. What did you just do to me?"

Slowly, Luis drew back. He released Paolo's cock from his sinful mouth and gazed up at Paolo, eyes red and wet. He'd always been beautiful, but in that moment, he had Paolo spellbound.

Paolo fought for breath and for balance as he struggled upright from where he'd slumped on the counter. He found Luis's face and tugged him close. Their lips met in a salty, sweet kiss, and it was as if they'd been together like this a dozen times. That kissing was their normal, not something they'd fallen into by drunken accident only yesterday.

On shaky legs, Paolo slid from the counter. Luis caught him but wavered enough for Paolo to know he was as blindsided as him. *Take it out of the kitchen.*

Ten minutes ago, the bedroom had seemed a world away. Suddenly, though, it was right there. Paolo yanked his jeans up enough that he could walk, then the bed hit the back of Luis's legs, and Paolo toppled them down. The teeny tiny part of his brain still functioning was loud enough for him to know fucking was off the table, but he needed something. He needed more. And so did Luis. He had to. You didn't give blowjobs like that without setting yourself on fire too.

Paolo broke the kiss but left them as they were, legs entangled, skin on skin, wrapped up in each other like old time lovers. "I didn't know this about you . . . that you were into blokes. Of everything the street says about you, never this."

Luis shrugged. "Bet no one ever said my brother was straight either. Ain't no one's business. Besides, you don't exactly wear a sandwich board yourself."

"Same reasons. I don't hide, but I don't care enough to broadcast it either."

"Are you gay?"

"No. Pan. My last boyfriend had more lacy knickers than jeans."

"For real?"

"For real. Boy, girl, everything in between. It's all good for me."

"Wow." Luis rolled onto his back. "That's so fucking hot."

"Is it?"

"Yeah. I've never found anyone who says the shit that's in my head before."

"You're pansexual?"

"If that's what it's called."

"You can call it whatever you like. It's your sexuality."

Luis sat up on his elbows. "I've never called it anything. And it's not that big of a secret, to be honest. Dante knows, he always has. I kept it off the street for the sake of anyone I was with, not because of *who* I was with."

"And were you?"

"What?"

"With anyone?"

"Before I went down?"

Paolo nodded. It was none of his business, but god, it felt like he'd catch fire if he didn't cram the Luis part of his brain to the rafters.

Luis sighed. "Not really. There was someone I messed around with for a while, but it was too complicated to keep doing it. After that, I'd go out of town to hook up, but nothing serious. I didn't want to pull anyone into the life I had back then."

"That's sensible."

"Maybe, but if I'd had someone to go home to, I might've been less reckless."

"Reckless?"

"Stupid. Whatever."

"That's not what I meant."

"It doesn't matter what you meant. I know what I was. What I am. I don't need you to tell me."

Luis spoke, as always, without fire and accusation. Just bland self-deprecation that made Paolo's blood boil for the wrong reasons.

He sat up too. In the murky light from the hallway, Luis seemed like an apparition. Paolo had to touch him to be sure he was there. His palm hit Luis's chest and ghosted over the smooth skin he found there. The tattoos were old, shadows in the dark. Paolo wondered what they meant but didn't ask. His fingers found the silver bar in Luis's nipple. He brushed his thumb over it.

Luis shivered, and goosebumps broke out over his skin. "I like that."

"Yeah?"

"Yeah."

"What else do you like?"

"Lots of things. I think."

"How long has it been?"

"Since what?"

Paolo replaced his thumb with his teeth, nipping gently, hands free to roam lower and unbutton Luis's jeans. "Don't be coy, mate. I'm asking if you fucked anyone in prison."

"Why not just say that then?"

"Cos I'm being coy."

"Different rules for you?"

"Nope. I'm just a twat."

"You're really not."

"Are you going to answer the question?"

"I didn't fuck anyone in prison, but . . ."

Paolo looked up. Luis was watching him, eyes heavy, cheeks flushed. "But what? Did you hook up with your cell mate?"

"One-eyed Joe? No. It wasn't an inmate."

"A guard? I thought that only happened on TV."

Luis snorted. "It happens all the time. Guards get horny for bad boys. It's cliched bullshit, but it worked for me back then."

"Man or woman?"

"Man."

"Did you love him?"

"What? No. I barely knew him. He asked me to suck him off, so I did, a lot, until I realised he thought he was too good to return the favour."

"He never did?"

"No."

"Wow. He sounds like a treat."

"He was an arsehole. But I was . . . I don't know. Desperate is too strong, but it was kind of like that. I wanted him to touch me. Like, craved it. Not from him in particular, but from anyone. He just happened to be my best hope."

"And it didn't pan out?"

Luis shook his head. "Not even a little bit."

"Was there anyone else?"

"No."

Paolo did the maths. "So is my blowjob-addled brain correct in assuming no one has made you come since *before* you went to prison six years ago."

"What makes you think I didn't score the second I came out?"

"I don't know. But I don't think you did. I think taking care of yourself, in any way whatsoever, was the last thing on your mind."

"You seem pretty sure of how my mind works."

"Am I wrong?"

"About what? My selflessness or lack of sex life?"

"Both."

Luis made a low noise in the back of his throat. "Why do you see me so well? I don't get it. No one else does."

"Maybe no one else is looking."

"That's too fucking true to contemplate right now."

He was right. Rolling around on Paolo's bed, clothes disappearing as fast as Paolo could strip them away, contemplating anything that wasn't making Luis shudder and groan wasn't going to happen. It had been a hell of a day, and it was turning into a hell of a night, but once Paolo had Luis exactly how he wanted him—naked, on his back, eyes wide with desire—nothing else mattered. He took Luis apart with his hands and mouth, drawing him into a climax that seemed to last for hours. Then, when Luis was done, Paolo came again, painting his belly.

They didn't shower. Sleep came too easily, and Paolo drifted away with Luis's head on his chest.

9

It was still dark when Luis woke up. He came to slower than usual and without the kickstart to his pulse. The shot of fear he'd never truly understood. Instead, he opened his eyes to the warmth of another body pressed against him from behind, strong arms wrapped around him, and morning wood digging into his back.

Paolo. He relaxed even more.

Everything was misty, like a dream, but the dick carving a hole in his spine was real. A smile formed even before Paolo's bedroom took shape. Luis was bone tired, his legs ached, and his eyes scratched like sandpaper, but god, he felt good. For the first time in fuck knew how long, he felt . . . alive.

He felt human.

Human enough that his bladder drove him out of bed and down the hall to Paolo's tiny bathroom.

Luis relieved himself and stumbled back to the bedroom. *You should go.*

But Paolo's sleeping form reeled him in. He hadn't moved. He was deeply asleep, dark hair a riot that made him even more gorgeous than normal. Luis lay down next to him and brushed it off his forehead. He traced the shadows beneath Paolo's eyes, wishing them away, and glanced around for something to cover him with. They hadn't made it into bed. Had passed out sticky and sweaty, kissing until they fell asleep.

Luis had never spent an entire night in a man's bed. Too busy with thug life for sleepovers. Perhaps he'd missed out on a hundred mornings like this, but he doubted it. He'd never been with anyone like Paolo. No one who saw him like Paolo did. Knew things without Luis having to say them. And fuck, *no one* had ever touched him like Paolo. Made him shout like that when he came, and the whole world had turned white. *Fucking-A, that shit was off the scale.*

Hot.

Addictive.

Luis wanted to wake Paolo up and do it all over again, but they were fast running out of time. Dawn was creeping in. Before long, Paolo would be awake, and work would take them away from the quiet sanctuary of his bedroom. Luis had learned to love working at the cafe, but there was something so tranquil about watching Paolo sleep, he didn't know how he'd ever stop. How he'd ever tear himself away and go back to the real world. The one with bacon sandwiches instead of blowjobs, and awkward customers instead of gentle kisses, and questions that splayed Luis open.

Somewhere on the bed, a phone began to vibrate, softly at first, but then louder, harder, with the added soundtrack of "*A Town Called Malice.*"

Luis found the phone and shut off the alarm.

Paolo still hadn't stirred. Luis considered leaving him to sleep a little while longer. Then he remembered the delivery, and the fact that despite exchanging earth shattering blowjobs, Paolo would probably freak if he woke up to find his keys had been lifted and Luis gone.

He settled for stroking Paolo's face until his eyelids started to flutter. Then he sat back in case Paolo had forgotten he was there.

Paolo's eyes slid open, heavy and dark. His gaze found Luis in a heartbeat, zeroed in and focussed before it zoned out again. "Damn. I thought you were real."

"I am real."

"Really? How come you stopped doing that thing with your thumb on my cheek?"

"You felt that?"

"I think so. Or I dreamt it, which backs up my theory that you're not real."

"I'm real." Luis brought his hand back to Paolo's face and rubbed his thumb over his cheekbone. "See?"

Paolo made a low sound and closed his eyes. "So last night really did get as out of hand as I remember?"

"Depends on your definition of out of hand. I probably have more scope for it than you."

Paolo cracked an eye open. "If you say so. What time is it?"

"Half four."

"Ugh. In my next life, I'm gonna have one of those burger vans outside the pubs. Late nights only."

"So you'd be going to bed around now?"

"Yeah, but I wouldn't have to get up till after *Eastenders*."

"You watch that shit?"

"Sometimes, when I visit Toni. He loves it."

Luis helped Paolo sit up. Like Luis, he was naked. His olive skin and soft, dark body hair were as gorgeous as they'd been last night when he'd had Luis's cock in his mouth. Fresh heat bloomed in Luis's gut, but they didn't have time to fool around—if Paolo even wanted to revisit what they'd done last night. They had a cafe to open.

They took separate showers. Paolo gave Luis a toothbrush and pressed a hooded sweat jacket into his hands before they left the flat with damp hair and shifty eyes. It was cold out. The hoodie was the closest to a coat Luis possessed, and he was glad of it, but it smelt of Paolo, and he was sorely unprepared for how that made him feel. For how his head spun with each breath, and every step they took towards the waiting cafe felt like a seismic shift to a dynamic that had been loaded, even before they'd rolled around on it.

Paolo was quiet. He kept his usual grouchy chatter to himself, but he walked close to Luis, their arms brushing from time to time, so Luis left him alone.

At the cafe, Paolo unlocked the back door and let them in. The fresh delivery was pulling up. Luis went inside and flipped the lights while Paolo signed for it, then set to work putting it away.

When he was done, he moved to the dishwasher to set it up for the day but found it already on and loaded with detergent and salt. He circled the rest of his morning jobs and found them completed too.

Puzzled, he searched out Paolo. He was sitting at his favourite table, scowling at the notebook he used to keep his accounts.

"You've done all my jobs," Luis said. "Why?"

Paolo kept his gaze down as he replied.

Luis frowned. "What?"

Paolo glanced up and winced. "Sorry. I said, I've done your jobs so you can do mine. I meant it when I said I didn't want you stuck on the dishwasher if you didn't have to be."

"You want me to, like, cook and shit?"

"If you can cook without the shit, that would be great. But yeah. If you're happy to do it?"

Luis chewed his bottom lip. Cooking for a few hours yesterday afternoon had gone well because he'd recognised most customers and had been able to guess their orders when he'd missed what they'd said. A busy breakfast service was something else. Luis could fry eggs till the cows came home, but what good was that if no one had asked for them in the first place?

Paolo rose from the table and was in Luis's face before he heard him coming. "What are you worried about?"

"I'm not worried."

"Liar."

"Yeah."

"So what is it?"

Luis turned his gaze to the floor. He'd mopped it twice yesterday and dried it by hand with paper towels. Was it clean enough? Did Paolo think he hadn't mopped it at all?

Paolo nudged him. Luis forced himself to meet his searching stare and not shrug him off. "I don't like taking orders. I miss things, then they walk away before I can ask them what it was. And I don't know what it was that I missed, so I look like a damn fool anyway."

"If you knew what you'd missed, you wouldn't have missed it, so that makes no sense."

"It does when you're me. I'm never sure if I've really missed something or I'm being paranoid."

"Oh." Paolo nodded slowly. "I've never thought about it like that. How about you cook, and I'll do the peopling?"

"What about the dishes?"

"I'll do them too."

"Why?"

"Because spending six days a week washing dishes isn't going to help you get a better job when the time comes. You need more tangible experience you can sell to another employer."

"I don't want another employer."

"Because you like washing dishes? Or you like your dick in my mouth?"

Luis blinked. "Um, both? Neither? I don't know. I just have no plans to get another job, unless this is you letting me go."

Paolo laughed. "I'm not letting you go. I just think it's better for *you* to do more while you're here than wash dishes all day, but I'm not going to make you cook if you don't want to."

"I don't mind. I like cooking."

"Now he tells me." Paolo rolled his eyes and returned to his accounts.

Luis left him to it and approached the grill. Lighting it was simple enough. He put the egg pans on to heat and filled the bread baskets for the toaster. Paolo had already brought out the sliced mushrooms and seasoned tomatoes. Luis checked the bacon and sausages he'd stashed in the front fridges last night and prepped the black pudding. *I'm ready . . . I think?*

Who the hell knew?

Luis poured coffee and took it to Paolo. "You usually make the tea."

"So where's yours?"

"Haven't made it yet."

"Don't forget."

"I won't."

Luis walked back to the grill, sensing Paolo's gaze on him. The urge to go back and kiss him was so strong he nearly tripped over his own feet, but a glance at the clock stopped him. It was opening time.

Paolo unlocked the door. The usual queue of builders from the site up the road was waiting, and they flowed into the cafe like a river of dust and hard hats. Orders came in thick and fast. Luis deciphered Paolo's scruffy handwriting and ploughed through them. From time to time, Paolo peered over his shoulder, but he said nothing, just took the food and delivered it. At least, Luis presumed he did. He was too busy to turn round.

It was after ten when the orders slowed enough to remind him what else Paolo did every morning. He cooked up two plates of leftover sausages and scrambled eggs and took them to the table.

Paolo was at the dishwasher, swearing at a stuck tray.

Luis reached around him and freed it. "That one's broken. It catches on the runners."

"Why didn't you chuck it away?"

"It doesn't belong to me."

Paolo muttered something Luis didn't mind missing. He pointed to the kitchen door. "Breakfast is ready."

Luis didn't wait for Paolo to respond. He retreated to the front and took the seat that left him facing the cafe entrance so he could watch for new customers coming in. He didn't hear Paolo coming, but it didn't matter because Paolo had stopped coming up behind him without warning. A soft hand on his back, a kicked chair. Something. Anything. Luis didn't have the heart to tell him the hairs standing up on the back of his neck always let him know Paolo was close.

Paolo brushed a hand over Luis's shoulder and slipped into his seat. Irritation clouded his handsome face, but Luis had learned not to take it personally. Everything annoyed Paolo—people, the weather, the radio. His near permanent scowl was part of his charm. Only his come-face came close.

Flustered, Luis tried not to think about it, but even grilling sixteen packs of bacon and thirty-eight sausages hadn't kept Paolo's naked self out of his thoughts. Not that Luis was complaining. Paolo's bed had proved a pleasant place to be.

Maybe too pleasant.

Luis wasn't looking forward to returning to his own.

Paolo kicked him under the table. "Tired?"

"Hmm?"

"Tired," Paolo repeated, a little louder. "Did you sleep okay?"

"Passed out, more like. It was a trip."

Paolo smirked. "Good. And I'm sorry about what I said earlier about you liking your dick in my mouth. What happened last night isn't relevant to your job here, so don't ever worry about that."

"I'm not worried."

"Are you going to tell me where you learned to cook for thirty people at a time?"

"You know where I learned."

"I'm not a mind reader."

"Nah, but you're clever, so I think you can figure out it's not something I picked up on the road."

Paolo's frown deepened, then cleared as comprehension dawned. "You cooked in prison?"

"In the canteen. You asked me if I had a job, remember? But I never got round to answering you."

Paolo sat back in his seat. He hadn't touched his breakfast, but then, neither had Luis. Who needed food when he had Paolo?

"Wow," Paolo said. "That makes sense. I don't know why I didn't think of it. What kind of stuff did you cook?"

"Nothing you'd want to eat. Most of it was packaged slop, but I did some courses a few years ago where we learned to cook other stuff, and I knew how to fry eggs before I went down. My mum wasn't much of a mum."

"Neither was mine. And my nonna was always working. If I wanted a hot dinner, I had to come here."

You were lucky. But Luis didn't say it. Paolo was rich in things Luis had never had, but that didn't make his life easy. And, he still looked annoyed.

Luis nudged him with his knee. "Why are you pissed off?"

"What makes you think I'm pissed off?"

"Everything about you."

"Very funny." Paolo schooled his features.

Luis laughed, but he still wanted to know.

Paolo sighed. "I'm annoyed with myself that I never asked you the right questions when I gave you the job. I made assumptions instead of realising you'd find it hard to talk about stuff you'd done in prison."

"How is any of that your fault?"

"Because it's me that did it all. Or didn't do it, depending on how you look at it."

"You're insane."

"Thanks."

"You are, though. How is it your fault I learnt my only life skills in the nick and would rather fucking die than tell you?"

"Because I'm an unapproachable, judgmental dickhead?"

"You're a judgmental dickhead, but nothing you assumed about me was wrong."

Paolo's frown deepened, but as he started to speak, the cafe door opened, and Luis's worst nightmare stepped over the threshold. He let loose a sigh of his own and cut Paolo off.

"Don't bother. I get the feeling I'm about to prove you were right all along."

————

Paolo took the breakfast plates to the kitchen and scraped the food they'd forgotten to eat into the bin. Luis had dragged his visitor around the back of the cafe. They were by the yard gate. Paolo tried not to stare, but morbid curiosity let him down. Who cared if a line was forming at the counter?

Not Paolo. Not while some fuckhead from Moss Farm was within breathing distance of the man he'd shared his bed with last night.

Not that a mutual blowjob exchange gave Paolo ownership of Luis, but he didn't give a fuck. He'd expected this day, but the weeks of nothing had lulled him into hoping it wouldn't happen. That Luis's old life had forgotten about him, and Luis had a chance of doing something different.

Paolo didn't know the face who'd showed up. It wasn't Dante Pope. But he was dressed like a road man, and even without the ludicrous swagger, the blacked-out car idling on the pavement round the front gave him away.

Scowling, Paolo dumped the plates in the sink. His

conscience told him to go back to work and mind his own damn business, but it was the same conscience that sent agitation sluicing through him and made him want to barge out of the back door and chin whoever it was that had aged Luis a decade in three and a half minutes.

Because that was how long it had been, and conscience or not, Paolo wasn't going to make it to five without causing a scene.

At least, that's what he told himself as he tore himself away from the window and went back to work. *Five minutes, and I'm telling that scumbag to get the fuck off my property.* But fifteen minutes passed, and he stayed where he was, serving customers at the till and making a mess of the grill Luis had kept spotless all day, until Luis eventually returned.

Paolo watched as he picked up his tongs and flipped six rashers of bacon as if he'd been doing it his whole life. And that he hadn't been gone for half an hour.

Leave it—

"What was all that about?" Paolo asked.

Luis cast him a flat stare. "I've been summoned."

"By who?"

"Who do you think?"

"Your brother?"

"Yup. Apparently he's upset I haven't paid him a royal visit."

"Are you going to go?"

"Fuck, no. I hate him."

Relief rippled through Paolo, along with a hefty dose of shame. He had no right to will Luis away from his own family. But, god, it felt good to know Luis didn't want whatever his brother was offering. And wrong. So fucking wrong. Luis was sweet and kind and funny. He didn't deserve to be alone in the world. "Isn't there anyone else? From before, I mean. I know you don't want to see your mum, but—"

"There's no one else."

Luis's tone left no room for argument. The conversation was dead. Luis took the grill back and spent the rest of the day cooking pristine, delicious plates of food in absolute silence, his face a mask of bland indifference as frustration ate away at Paolo's gut. Luis was a man of few words at the best of times, but his quiet grin often spoke for him, his gentle smile. The little things he did to make Paolo's life a hundred times easier.

His shifts finished at three. He often hung around till after closing, helping Paolo shut down the cafe, ignoring Paolo's reminders that he couldn't pay him for the extra time. *"I don't care. You pay me enough already."*

As if. Luis was still wrestling with the bank to get his account unlocked, so Paolo had yet to pay him at all. He tried to make up for it by sending Luis home with dinner every night, but that hadn't happened since the night they'd first kissed. Other things had happened instead. Things that erased Paolo's common sense and made him want to shut the whole world out so he could take Luis home and pretend that rolling around in his bed was all that mattered. *You don't have to do that. You can take him out. Buy him a beer. Let him talk.* Resolved, Paolo shut down the dishwasher and wandered out of the kitchen.

But Luis had already gone.

———

After hanging around the cafe later than necessary to see if Luis would come back, Paolo went home. It was Tuesday, the day his cousin visited Toni and Nonna so Paolo could have a night to himself. Sometimes he went to the supermarket or the pub to catch up with the handful of people he vaguely called friends, but with Luis on his mind, he went straight home. He took a shower and searched the cupboards and fridge for dinner. There wasn't much, just rice, chicken, and a jar of curry sauce that had seen better days.

He left the saucepan simmering on the stove and decamped to the couch with his laptop to pay bills and catch up on admin. Luis's wages were stacked up in a separate account, minus the cash he'd set aside to pay him to pay him at the end of the week. In the grand scheme of things, it wasn't much, but to Luis, they were everything. Paolo topped them up, including a raised hourly rate for the time he'd managed the cafe alone, but even with the added cash, it didn't seem enough. Agitated, he shut the laptop and drifted to the big window that looked out over the city. Luis was out there somewhere. Perhaps he'd gone home, but Paolo's gut didn't believe it. The road man drive-by had changed everything. He didn't know how, but it had.

Unable to rest, Paolo turned the stove off, pocketed Luis's cash, and left the flat. He walked into the wind, hood up, hiding his face in his coat. On every street corner, the kids Dante Pope used to move his drugs rolled around on their bikes, eyeing every soul that passed them.

But they ignored Paolo, and for once he was glad to be a local. He wasn't in the mood to tell a baby-faced slinger to go fuck themselves or deal with consequences. It had been a while since the cafe's last broken window.

Luis lived on Crawley Road in the bedsits the council had made out of the tatty terraced houses. The exact address was in Paolo's phone so he could register Luis's tax, but he hadn't memorised it, and as he approached the flats, he didn't check. Instead, he forced himself to stare at the windows, some lit, some not, and imagine Luis safe inside, cooking his own dinner, standing under a hot shower, perhaps even tucked up in bed, and maybe he wasn't alone. Maybe he was—

"What are you doing here?"

Paolo spun around. Luis stood behind him, leaning on a lamp post, his hair messy and damp. He looked tired, but not in the way of a man who'd been up all night doing anything fun. It was a different kind of weary, one that haunted a man and weighed him down. "I was taking a walk," Paolo said.

Luis's brow ticked up. "Round here? You're brave."

"Stupid, actually. I was going to drop your cash off too."

"You're walking these streets with a pocket of cash? Fucking-A." Luis pushed off the lamp post. "Yeah, you are stupid. Why didn't you just give it to me tomorrow?"

Because you left without saying goodbye, and I was worried about you. Paolo doled out his best Luis-style shrug. "Fancied a walk. And I thought you might need it. You've had no money since you got out."

"Haven't needed any. You feed me every day."

"What about bills?"

"Not till next week. And I had enough cash from my discharge grant to top up the electric."

"Fair enough." Paolo fished the small roll of bills from his pocket and held it out.

Luis pushed his hand down and hissed through his teeth. "Not out here. Are you fucking nuts? One side will do you for dealing while the other will smash you up for slinging on their turf."

Paolo rolled his eyes but let his hand drop all the same. "Whatever. You want me to take it home and give it to you tomorrow, or are you gonna invite me in?"

"You want to see my shithole of a flat?"

"I want you to have your money so you can take care of yourself."

"And give you your coat back, huh?"

"What? No. That's not why." Luis was still wearing Paolo's hoodie. He started to take it off. Paolo gripped his arms and forced them down. "Stop it. I don't want it back."

"Then why are you really here?"

"Because—" Paolo pursed his lips. What the fuck was he about to say? That he couldn't stand the thought of Luis being alone despite the fact that they'd only spent one whole night together? That he missed him and wanted to take him to bed? If Luis didn't think he was a lunatic by now, he would then. "Because I was worried about you. You left without saying anything."

"Yeah, sorry about that. I had something I had to do."

"Like seeing your brother?"

"No."

"Then what?"

Luis shrugged. "What do you care? I already told that prick Dante sent not to come up on me at work. It won't happen again."

Paolo blinked. It was like talking to someone else. Like talking to the Luis Pope he'd first imagined when he'd looked up to see him waiting at the counter. "That wasn't what I was worried about, but whatever. There's your money, bro. See you in the morning."

He tossed Luis's cash at his feet and walked away.

Silence followed him, then footsteps, fast and heavy. Rough hands grabbed him and spun him around. Expecting a mugger, Paolo hit out. Luis took the shove to his chest and held firm. "You fucking lunatic."

The echo of his own thoughts brought Paolo back to reality. He stopped struggling. "You're the one wrestling with me in the middle of the street."

"Only because I don't want you to leave like this."

"Like what?"

"Like a crazy person who throws money at people."

"It's your money."

"So? Give it to me, don't throw it at me."

"You're annoying."

"Everything annoys you."

Paolo rolled his eyes. "Doesn't make you less annoying."

Luis cracked a fleeting smile. He loosened his grip on

Paolo, then seemed to change his mind and held him tighter, frowning again. "I don't want you to leave at all, but I don't want to show you my shitty bedsit either."

"Why? My flat's shitty too."

"Trust me, it's not."

"Who do you think I am? Like, really? Some arsehole who looks down his nose at people? Luis, mate. The reason I knew who *you* were is because we're from the same place. Why would I judge you?"

Luis searched Paolo's face, though for what, Paolo had no idea. He waited, perversely enjoying the roughness of Luis's hold, until Luis seemed to find what he was looking for. "Come on, then."

He let Paolo go and spun on his heel. Paolo followed him to a terraced house in the middle of the row and through a battered front door. Muffled music rattled the dingy hallway. Luis nodded to a door at the end. "I'm on the ground floor."

"At the back or the front?"

"The back."

There was an odd reassurance in knowing he could've stood on the street all night and still not caught a glimpse of Luis. That if Luis had been home, he'd never have known Paolo's madness. But then, he was a perceptive motherfucker. Perhaps he'd have taken one look at Paolo the next day and figured it out.

Luis unlocked the door at the end of the hallway and waved Paolo into a tiny bedsit that was spotlessly clean.

And empty. Only a small divan bed took up the corner of the main room, neatly made with blue sheets. The bag

Luis had carried when he'd first drifted into the cafe was in the corner, open with a small stack of clean clothes. There was nothing else, no TV, stereo, or furniture, just a storage heater that looked a hundred years old.

Through another door was a kitchen area with a single-ring hob, a fridge, and a toaster. Paolo frowned. "Where's your washing machine?"

"In the bathroom."

"What?"

"It's in the bathroom," Luis repeated. "Go look if you don't believe me."

Paolo looked, and when he saw the washing machine tucked in next to the shower, he laughed. "Wow. That's as good a use of space if I've ever seen it. Does it work?"

"Yeah, it's noisy as fuck, though. So I don't use it at night."

Paolo turned his back on the bizarre bathroom and re-joined Luis in his kitchen. There was a pot on the stove. "What's in there?"

"Beans."

"What kind of beans?"

"Kidney beans, with chilli sauce and bacon."

"Show me?"

"Erm, okay." Luis lifted the lid of the pot. Deep red beans were sitting in a fiery sauce of tomatoes, chilli flakes, and sautéed bacon. It was as good a dinner as Paolo had ever seen, and his empty belly rumbled.

Luis laughed. "Hungry?"

"Of course. I'm Italian and I haven't eaten for more than an hour."

Luis had bread and a tub of butter. He ladled his bean concoction into two mugs and passed Paolo a spoon. "Sorry, I only had one fork, and I broke it fixing the fuse box."

"I'm filing that away for the next time something blows at the cafe." Paolo followed Luis out of the kitchen and sat opposite him, cross legged, on the floor.

The beans were good . . . so good, Paolo finished his in ten seconds flat and sat back against the wall while Luis ate. "This place isn't so bad."

Luis snorted around a mouthful of bread. "It's not the worst place I've ever slept, but I wouldn't call it home."

"Not planning on staying then?"

"I can make all the plans I like. Doesn't mean I'm going anywhere."

"I know that feeling."

"Where would you want to go?"

Paolo sighed. "Dunno. Never stopped to think about it."

"Because of your grandparents?"

"Maybe. Or maybe it's me. Running the cafe meant I never had to make any choices about my future, so I don't have any dreams."

Luis ate the last of his beans and set the mug on the floor. "I've never had any either. When I was running for Dante, making it to the next day was all I was aiming for, and inside, time just stops, you know? I didn't even care that much about getting out."

"For real?"

"Yeah. It wasn't like I had anything to come back to."

"Not even your brother?"

"Fuck my brother."

"So you still haven't seen him?"

"No."

Luis got up and gathered the mugs and spoons. He took them into the kitchen.

He's lying. Paolo stood slowly and trailed after him like a man walking to the gallows.

Luis was at the sink, head bowed, shoulders heavy.

Paolo stepped up behind him and wound his arms around Luis's waist. Despite the chasm between them, they fit together like a perfect puzzle with no missing pieces. Paolo knocked his head on Luis's spine, breathing him in. "I should go."

"I don't want you to."

"Why?"

"Because I feel better when you're close."

"Better than what?"

"Than everything."

It made no sense. But nothing about how Luis made Paolo feel ever did. He pressed up tighter against him, letting desire seep from deep in his gut and overcome everything else. Doubts faded. Fear lost its grip. Paolo slid his hands beneath Luis's waistband and lower. "I'll stay . . . for a little while."

10

Luis's kitchen had a small window, no blind. There was an alleyway behind the building where slingers kept their stashes. Any one of them could've glanced in and seen Luis hunched over the counter, jeans bunched at his thighs, but he didn't care. He *couldn't* care, about anything while Paolo was on his knees behind him.

Not even the fact he'd told him a bare-faced lie.

"Sup, my brother? You've been hiding from me."

Paolo pushed his tongue inside Luis again, deeper this time. Luis screwed his eyes shut. Sweet sensation rocked him, and he moaned, but it wasn't loud enough to drown out Dante's mocking voice.

"It's good to see you, bro. Manor hasn't been the same without you. Are you ready to talk business, or are you still playing lacky at that greasy spoon?"

"So what if I am?" Luis fought to keep his aggression down. *"You don't need me up in your shit. I'm the one that gets caught, remember?"*

"Yeah, but it looks bad on me to have you dicking around in town when you should be with me. Come back, man. Hero's welcome."

"I don't want a hero's welcome. I want to get on with my life."

"You don't want to do that with me? Making all the Ps you could ever need?"

"No."

Dante had taken the rejection well. His bland smile had hidden his sneer, and he'd let Luis leave with no indication that he'd see him again, but Luis knew him better than anyone. Perhaps better than he knew himself. Dante Pope was king of his castle, and no one told him no. Not even his brother.

Especially not his brother. Luis had bought himself time, nothing else. And who the fuck knew how much. A month. A week.

A day.

Luis groaned again, pushing back against Paolo's probing tongue. He hadn't been rimmed in so long, he'd forgotten he ever had. And he'd *never* had someone explore him the way Paolo was right then. "Fuck, that's so fucking good."

Paolo let out a low laugh and snaked a hand around Luis's hip to his cock. He squeezed with a light pressure that almost sent Luis to his knees. "Come on. Let's take this to your bed."

Stumbling, Luis straightened up and took Paolo's outstretched hand. Trust flowed between them, a trust Luis didn't deserve. But Dante's voice had quieted, cowed by the sensory overload of Paolo and his wicked tongue, and Luis was done with coherent thought until he was alone again.

Paolo pushed him down on the bed, face first. "On your knees."

Luis shivered, obeying the gentle command without question. He pressed his chest into the mattress and spread his legs, hoping Paolo heard the words he couldn't bring himself to say. *You can't trust me, but I trust you.*

Paolo rubbed Luis's back and unbuttoned his own jeans. Luis's pulse quickened. His body was crying out for Paolo to fuck him, but his head wasn't ready for the kind of sex he knew Paolo was offering. The kind that took a man, turned him inside out, and put him back together as someone else.

Fear threatened the bliss of having Paolo so close to him. He sucked in a breath. "I—"

"Shh." Paolo hunched over him and kissed his spine. "Nothing's gonna happen. I just want to feel you."

He slid his cock along Luis's wet crease so slowly Luis legitimately fucking whimpered. *What is it about him that breaks me apart so fuckin' fast?* He had zero clue. All he knew was that Paolo's rock-hard dick gliding over his slick flesh made him lose his god damn mind. He arched his spine, desperate for more but afraid of what it meant. Paolo kept up his torture for a few moments longer, then flipped Luis onto his back.

The abrupt change in position shocked Luis back to reality. He gazed at Paolo, taking in every facet of him, from his big dick, to his lean abs and perfect chest. His inky curls were a riot, his skin sheened with sweat. And his eyes . . . *fuck, I could live in them.*

Luis's body thrummed with desire. He'd never wanted anyone like this. He wasn't ready for Paolo to fuck him, but he needed something—anything to quell the fire raging in him. "I need you."

Paolo gripped his cock, pleasuring himself. His lashes fluttered. "Right back at you."

He fell forwards, bracing himself with his hands either side of Luis's head. Kissing came to them like breathing now, soft and sweet, hard and demanding, they'd mastered it all. Luis lost himself in Paolo's lips and tongue, all the while wondering how he'd ever lived without them. How he'd lasted twenty-eight years without Paolo's kiss. Dante faded away, as if he'd never existed. Stress, fatigue, fear, all eclipsed by the knot of pleasure Paolo had tied in his gut.

Paolo's fingers found the sweet spot of heat his tongue had searched for deep inside Luis, while his other hand jacked Luis's cock. The double-edged pleasure was unbearable. His shuddering groans seemed to belong to someone else. He dug his blunt nails into Paolo's shoulders and spread his legs wider.

"You're gonna make me come like a fucking train."

"Do it." Paolo worked his dick harder. "I want to see you, then I want to come down your throat."

He had a way of speaking filth like no other. His voice wrapped around the words as if he spoke them every day, so familiar and warm, but at the same time, laced with a potency that shoved Luis off the cliff.

The knot in his belly unravelled, whipping through

him like a firestorm. His body jerked, chasing the twist of Paolo's fingers and the friction of his fist. It was nowhere near enough, but far too much. A jackhammer hit his nerves, and he came with a strangled yell.

Paolo kissed him through it and slowly reclaimed his hands. His dick was still rock-hard, and Luis wanted it in his mouth.

Breathless, he fell back and tugged Paolo over him.

Paolo straddled his chest and brought his cock to Luis's mouth. He gripped the ancient headboard screwed to Luis's divan bed and eased between Luis's lips. His thighs quivered, and only his teeth digging into his bottom lip kept his sinful mouth from hanging open.

Luis slid his hands over Paolo's strong legs, squeezing the soft flesh he found at the top as he urged Paolo on. Salty warmth coated his tongue. He opened his throat, and Paolo came with a loud groan, fast and hard.

It seemed to go on forever, but just when Luis thought he'd never breathe again, Paolo slipped out of his mouth and collapsed in a heap beside him.

Luis reached for him without conscious thought and pulled him close. The bedsit was cold, but the heat of what had passed between them kept them warm enough for now. He buried his face in Paolo's messy hair, breathing him in, clinging to the dream. *I want him forever.* But Luis couldn't have him forever. They had only this moment.

———

Paolo fell asleep. Luis wrestled with the duvet until it was tucked around them and contemplated if he'd ever bring himself to wake him and walk him home. Paolo felt so good pressed naked against him that he doubted it, but he didn't want Paolo to wake up cold either. Either way, Luis couldn't resist a few minutes of listening to Paolo's soft, deep breaths. It calmed Luis like nothing else, and he clung to the feeling as his mind came back to life.

You shouldn't have gone to see Dante.

But what choice had he had? Sending muscle to the cafe had been a clear message: *Come to me before I come to you.* And if there was anything worse than random road men walking up on Paolo's place, it was Dante doing it himself. Dante ruled his crew with fear, and he was sharp enough to notice when someone didn't respect that fear. Luis would play his game a thousand times if it kept him from Paolo's door. *You should leave. Get another job and get out of Paolo's life. What reason would Dante have to visit him then?*

None. But Luis was too selfish to walk away. He needed Paolo like he needed air. He'd drown without him, even if they never laid hands on each other again. No one saw him like Paolo did.

Eventually, Luis dozed off, and he woke the next morning, once again, to Paolo's alarm. It was the second whole night they'd spent together and the second morning Luis had spent trying to wake Paolo. *Dude sleeps like the dead.* It was cute as fuck, from the way Paolo hid his face under the pillow, to his childish annoyance when he finally woke up.

He scowled at Luis from beneath his heavy eyes. "Time is it?"

"Time to get up."

"As in time for work, or time for you to kick me out of your bed?"

"I'd never kick you out of my bed. You make it a nice place to be."

"Stop being sweet. It's too early for me to start crying."

With his face still crinkled from sleep, it was hard to tell if he was joking. All Luis knew was that he was fucking adorable, and as long as Paolo was in his shitty second-hand bed, he never wanted to get up.

Shame Paolo's alarm had other ideas.

Luis gave Paolo a toothbrush. "It's from Pound Stretchers. Sorry if it's shit."

Paolo rolled his eyes and ambled into the bathroom. He was back in two minutes flat with wet hair and a towel around his waist. "It's fucking cold in here. Do those heaters work?"

Luis waited for Paolo to hand him the towel before he shrugged and made his escape. He jumped in and out of the shower even quicker than Paolo and shivered as he dried off and found his last set of clean clothes.

Paolo was already dressed and still scowling at the storage heaters. "Thought you said you had gas?"

"I do, but it only runs the water."

"No central heating?"

"Not from the boiler, no."

Paolo got up from Luis's bed and crouched in front of the nearest storage heater. He opened the dial. "It's not turned on."

"I know."

"Why not?"

"I don't need them on."

"Luis, it's freezing in here. I know you haven't got Italian blood to keep warm, but you're not a fucking polar bear."

He rarely said Luis's name. They were together so often, just the two of them, there was no need. Luis liked the way his gravelly tone wrapped around it, even if he was making bullshit analogies. "They're expensive to run. And they don't get hot for hours, so I'm leaving again by the time they start working anyway."

Paolo fiddled with the dials. "You need to keep the output turned up during the winter."

"Okay, but I'm going to be out all day, so I don't want it on now, do I?"

"That's not how they—never mind." Paolo flicked the power switch on the wall. "Turn it on at the wall when you're at home, all right? Being cold all the time isn't a fucking joke."

Luis wondered how he knew. They'd shared a childhood without ever speaking to each other, but Luis had no idea when Paolo's parents had died, if he'd ever lived with them, and if he had, what it had been like. He wanted to know. Probably. Maybe. But then knowing for sure that Paolo had suffered wasn't something he wanted to live with.

Yeah, cos it's all about you.

They left the bedsit. Luis almost made himself leave Paolo's hoodie behind, but even with Paolo walking beside him, he was still addicted to its scent. He zipped it up to his nose and breathed deep while Paolo picked up stray cans and bottles and dumped them in the bins they passed.

It was a longer walk to the cafe from Luis's place. They arrived fifteen minutes later than usual, with no time for tea and a chat before they opened.

"You can cook," Paolo said.

"Okay."

"You don't have to."

Luis shrugged. "I don't mind."

"You should mind."

"Why? You're the boss."

"That doesn't take away your right to make decisions."

Luis hated it when Paolo said shit like that. It never made any sense. However many nights they'd spent together—a grand total of two so far—Paolo *was* his boss. To pretend otherwise was just fucking weird.

He took his place at the grill and took the filters out of the extractor fan to soak them in disinfectant.

Paolo peered over his shoulder. "I thought you did that yesterday morning?"

"So? You don't do it every day?"

"Not since Nonna retired. She'd like you."

"If you say so."

"I do."

Paolo looked as though he wanted to say more, but the cafe door opened and the first of the steady stream of builders walked in. Luis kept his back to them and cleaned the filters in record time. He refitted them as Paolo delivered the first breakfast orders. Paolo leant across Luis and wedged them onto the tab. He smelt of Luis's cheap apple shampoo and, yet, still of himself. Of the scent that kept Luis up some nights. After an evening spent touching Paolo with abandon, it was odd not to press forwards and bury his face in his neck. To breathe him in and let his hands roam his smooth olive skin.

Disquiet replaced heat and bloomed in Luis's gut.

Paolo glanced at him. "Okay?"

"Yup."

"Sure about that? You look like you're about to throw up."

Awesome. If that was how Luis appeared when he was fighting the urge to jump Paolo and rip his clothes off, fuck knew what he looked like when they were in bed together. "I'm fine."

He took the order slips and turned his back on Paolo too.

The morning stretched out. Luis cooked every order Paolo put in front of him and waited for his nerves to fade, but they didn't. Every whine and slam of the front door rattled his bones. Every car pulling up outside. Every voice he didn't recognise calling over the counter.

He craved the relative safety of the dishwasher. The anonymity. *That makes no fucking sense either. You'd still have to come out to clear the tables.* But at least he'd be able to see. At the grill, with his back to the front door and his busted left ear, maybe he did want to puke after all.

The breakfast rush petered out. Luis took his chance and ducked into the kitchen. Paolo wasn't there. Relief and disappointment fought for dominance.

Relief won out. Luis sucked in a deep breath that

rattled his chest, anxiety he hadn't felt in weeks awakening like a pissed off dragon. *Keep busy. Keep busy.* A stack of dishes was waiting by the dishwasher. Luis flew through them, cleaned out the dishwasher filters, and topped up the detergent, rinse aid, and salt.

Mushrooms sat on the prep counter. He sliced them, along with an extra tray of black pudding, but couldn't bring himself to take them out front.

He set them by the door and returned to the dishwasher.

Paolo appeared at the back door, phone pressed to his ear. He eyed Luis over his coffee cup as he gulped down the contents.

Luis looked away.

Paolo stepped up behind him. Luis's skin jumped, anticipating his touch, and it came slowly, as Paolo slid his arms around Luis's waist. "You wanna stay in here?"

How does he know? Luis closed his eyes. "Yeah. Sorry, I just—"

"Don't worry about it." Paolo pressed a kiss between Luis's shoulder blades, his lips barely grazing the thin cotton of Luis's T-shirt. "I got you."

He disappeared, taking a piece of Luis's heart with him and leaving Luis to ponder the trigger of the agitation prickling his skin.

Dante flashed into his mind. Luis pushed him away, but as he had Luis's entire fucking life, he wouldn't quit. He never did. Sending muscle to the cafe had just been the start, but of what, Luis had no idea. How bad did Dante want him back? It wasn't beyond him to play with Luis for fun, but what if he was serious enough to come looking for him again? To take it out on the cafe—on Paolo—if he didn't get his own way?

He'd done worse, and so had Luis, at Dante's bidding. There were no boundaries. No limits. No ceiling on what Dante would do to get what he wanted.

Luis's heart stuttered like a broken clock.

Paolo came back into the kitchen. He gripped Luis's shoulders and turned him round. "You wanna go home?"

"No."

"You sure? It's my fault you got no sleep."

"I slept."

"Then what is it? Is whatever's going down between us fucking with your head? Cos we can stop anytime you like. No hard feelings, I swear."

Luis's heart did another scraping flip. This was his chance to put a safe distance between them. To make them employee and boss before Dante got wind of something more. But he couldn't do it. Paolo kept him upright. Luis had only truly known him a few weeks, but the notion of living without him, in any capacity, left him weak for all the wrong reasons. "I don't want to stop."

"Okay." Paolo nodded slowly. "But will you at least go home and get some rest? It's fucking with *my* head to see you so tired. I don't do guilt well, even when it comes from something as hot as you."

Leaving him felt like the end of the world, but Paolo possessed an authority Luis couldn't ignore. The kind of authority that had him on his knees in the bedroom. Luis left and went home, failure like acid in his veins. He let himself into the bedsit, locked the doors, and drew the one pair of curtains he owned.

Darkness wrapped around him. On the kitchen counter, his phone buzzed.

Expecting Paolo, Luis picked it up. A message from an unsaved number flashed up on the screen.

Unknown number: *don't 4get abt me*

Luis stared at the message for a long time before he deleted it and put his phone in the fridge.

11

Paolo: *u get home okay?*
  Luis: *yea*

Paolo: *take tomorrow and thursday off. i'll pay you x*
  Luis: *u don't need to do that*
  Paolo: *i do if i don't wanna be a sweatshop boss*
  Luis: *dramatic*
  Paolo: *italian*

Paolo: *had enough of this shit for one day. wanna have dinner later? i'll cook something without bacon, i swear*

Paolo: *or not, i'm easy. just lemme know if ure coming in tomorrow x*

Paolo gave Luis the next day off, and the one after that. He half expected him to show up anyway, but when he didn't, Paolo ran the cafe alone and marvelled how he'd ever managed without Luis.

It was carnage. Dishes piled up. Tables went uncleared. By two o'clock on the second day, he ran out of steam. He shut the cafe early and went home with no regrets, except that he hadn't given Luis a key and asked him to let himself in.

He took a shower and fell asleep, naked, on his bed. It was dark when he woke, and the message he'd sent to Luis before he'd left the cafe had gone unanswered. Frowning, Paolo pulled up the message thread between them. As they were together most days, it was short, a grand total of twelve messages, and Luis wasn't exactly wordy, but he always replied. Every message, until this one.

Luis didn't like talking on the phone. Paolo didn't know if it was because of his damaged hearing or something else, but calling him felt wrong. So he didn't. He stared at his blank phone screen for a full hour, and then left the flat, intending to head the opposite direction to Luis's bedsit.

Fifteen minutes later, he buzzed Luis's door, shivering in the cold wind that rattled the uncovered porch. There was no answer. Paolo buzzed once more for luck, then admitted defeat and gave up.

Halfway down the road, his phone beeped.

Luis: *was that u at my door?*
　　Paolo: *yeah*
　　Luis: *come back?*
　　Luis: *please?*

As if Paolo could refuse.

He didn't even want to.

Hood up against the wind, he spun around and booked it back to Luis's building. The exterior door was cracked open. Paolo gave it a cautious push and stepped into the dark hallway. There was light at the end. Paolo followed it and slipped through Luis's open front door.

Luis reached over him and shut it. Bolted it. "Hey."

"Hey yourself."

Paolo ran his gaze over Luis, taking in his rumpled hair, unshaven jaw, and bare chest. *Man alive, how does he make sweatpants look so good?* Not kissing him was impossible. So Paolo didn't even try. He tugged Luis to him and brushed their lips together, once, twice, three times, with just enough pressure to make himself dizzy. Then he remembered why he'd come and pulled back. "You didn't answer my messages. Everything okay?"

"Yeah. Sorry. I didn't get them until just now. My phone was annoying me, so I, uh, put it somewhere else."

A dozen responses bubbled up Paolo's throat, but he swallowed them down. Luis had opened the door. That was enough. "So," he said. "I didn't actually mean to drop by, but here I am. But I can't stay. I gotta go see Toni. Are you coming in tomorrow?"

Luis nodded. "Yeah. Definitely."

"You sure? Take some more time if you need it."

"I don't. I didn't need this time, just figured you wanted me to take it."

"I did, but not for my benefit."

"Okay."

"Okay." Paolo let his hands slide from Luis's bare skin. Instinct told him to let it go, to leave Luis alone in whatever he was dealing with. But he turned to leave and his heart rebelled.

He turned back. "You wanna go somewhere with me?"

Luis stared at him for a long moment, then shrugged his glorious shoulders. "I'll go anywhere with you."

———

Toni had been asking to meet Luis for a while, but Paolo took him to Nonna first, on the bus, half an hour outside of the city. It was a journey Paolo had taken a thousand times, but with Luis squashed against him in a pair of seats at the back, it felt brand new.

Luis sat by the window, gazing out like a child on a school trip. Paolo watched him, fascinated. "Anyone would think you'd never been out."

No answer was forthcoming. He assumed Luis hadn't heard him and let it go. Then Luis sighed and turned to face him. "I haven't been out of the city since the day the police picked me up. I haven't seen a field since 2014."

Nice one, P. Could you be any more ignorant? "Sorry, I never thought about it like that."

"Why would you? You're not a criminal."

"Neither are you. You're reformed, right?"

Luis snorted and swung his attention back to the window.

Paolo nudged him. "Why the cynicism? Are you up to no good when you're not in my bed?"

"I've been in your bed once. That leaves plenty of time for trouble."

"I still don't believe it."

"Doesn't matter what you believe. It doesn't change who I am."

"Then you should've said that to me when I was judging you just for existing."

"Would you have listened?"

"No, but that says more about you than it does about me."

Luis said nothing for real this time. Paolo leaned on him but resisted the urge to close his eyes and doze. He'd made that mistake before and missed his stop by fifty miles.

Nonna's nursing home was in a leafy commuter town,

attached to an Anglican church. The entrance was next to the graveyard, and Luis froze at the gate. "I hate graveyards."

"Then don't look." Paolo grabbed his hand and tugged him forwards.

He didn't let go, and neither did Luis.

At the reception desk, a nurse glanced at their joined hands and smiled. Paolo ignored her and signed him in and Luis as a guest.

Nonna's room was on the second floor. "She doesn't walk anymore. Sometimes I take her out if there's a wheelchair knocking about, but she hates them, so we don't do it much."

"How often do you come here?"

"Twice a week, sometimes three if I can manage it. I see Toni more because he's closer, and . . ."

"And what?"

Paolo pressed the button for the lift with more force than strictly necessary. "He knows I'm there."

Luis squeezed his hand. He offered no bullshit words of comfort, and Paolo's affection for him expanded its reach, etching a permanent place for itself on his soul.

"I've never done this with anyone else," he said.

"Done what?" Luis squeezed his hand again. "Rode in a lift?"

"No, I've never brought anyone here. My cousin comes once a week, but I don't see him cos sometimes it's the only night I get to myself, you know? I can't be arsed to talk to him."

"I feel like that about most people."

"Even your family?"

"Especially my family."

"Sorry. I'm full of stupid questions today."

"You look tired."

"Yeah, well. I'm not used to running around the cafe by myself all day anymore. A month with you has erased three years of stamina."

Luis smirked, but the lift arrived before he could say whatever was on his mind.

They rode it to the second floor. Nonna's room was right in front of the lifts. Her door was open. Paolo could already see she was fast asleep, and he was glad of it. Luis's hand in his made him feel strong, but he wasn't in the mood to talk in circles with an audience. It begged the question of why he'd brought Luis along at all, but he wasn't in the mood to contemplate that either, so he busied himself straightening Nonna's room.

Luis took a seat in the corner. He watched Paolo bustle around, his watchful presence, as ever, a comfort, not an intrusion. Paolo had brought Nonna clean handkerchiefs. Luis took them from him and folded them into perfect triangles. "Where does she keep them?"

Paolo jerked his head at the dresser. "In the drawer."

Luis got up and opened the drawer. He placed the handkerchiefs inside and withdrew a framed photograph of Paolo and Toni. "When was this taken?"

"Judging by my tragic step cut, sometime in the nineties."

"I had one of those too, but I shaved it off when my mum wasn't looking."

"Was your hair blond when you were a kid?"

"Yeah, like bright strawberry blond. I had red cheeks too, like a cartoon."

"Where did your dog tags come from?"

Luis turned back to the drawer. "They're my dad's."

"Is he dead?"

"For a long time now."

"How did he die? Was he a soldier?"

"Yeah. He was killed in Bosnia when I was little."

"I'm sorry."

Luis put the photo back without asking why it was tucked away in a drawer and not proudly displayed, as if he already knew how much it scared Nonna to be watched over by faces she didn't always recognise. "It's okay. I never really knew him. It was harder for Dante."

"Why doesn't he wear the tags then?"

"Can't remember."

If the tells Paolo had imagined in Luis were correct, he was lying. But Nonna stirred before he could second guess every twitch of Luis's eyebrows, and not even Luis could distract him from that.

———

Nonna had one of those days where she didn't know who Paolo was. She called him Guiseppe and asked him to take her dancing. Paolo played along, as he always did. It was easier than forcing reality on her.

Didn't stop her figuring out that Paolo had it bad for

Luis, though. When they finally left her to it, Paolo had blushed more times than a shy bride.

Visiting Toni was easier. He knew Luis's face. Welcomed it and him, as if Paolo brought hot guys to see him all the time.

He didn't. But that didn't stop Paolo imagining a different life, one where Toni and Nonna got to grow old together in their garden flat, serving dinner at the battered kitchen table where Nonna had taught Paolo to hand roll pasta. There'd have been a place for Luis at that table if he'd wanted it.

Paolo wanted it, even if it was nothing but a dream.

They took the bus back from Toni's care home. Paolo sat by the window. Luis slumped down beside him and lolled his head on Paolo's shoulder. He looked asleep, though it was hard to tell. On the nights they'd spent together, Paolo had always knocked out first and woken up last. He wished it was one of those nights now, so he could absorb every moment of Luis so peaceful. Stroke his face and tangle his fingers in his silky hair without the distraction of making each other come.

Not that Paolo was complaining about that. Being naked with Luis was cloud nine territory. Problem was, he never wanted to come down.

The bus passed where Luis would get off if he was going home. He didn't stir, and Paolo didn't rouse him. At some point, he'd have to take a breath and figure out what the hell they were doing, but not yet. Their stolen nights together were too precious. Paolo couldn't give them up.

Not yet.

12

Luis hadn't been home in days. Every morning he rolled out of Paolo's bed and down the road to work, and each night, he rolled straight back in. Some evenings he went with Paolo to visit his grandparents; others, he stayed in Paolo's flat, figuring out how to use his TV and trying to pretend that immersing himself so entirely in Paolo's life was a good idea.

It wasn't a good idea. Luis had ignored Dante's text, and there'd been no others, but the sense of borrowed time was so strong, Luis woke each day feeling like it was the end of the world. Paolo's arms around him helped, but too soon, it was always time to get up and face the day.

He hadn't cooked for days either. Paolo never asked him why or forced him away from the dishwasher, but on the fourth Saturday since Luis's release, it was time for him to learn the way of the pasta pot.

"You don't have to," Paolo said. "I'm thinking of jacking it in anyway. I need more days off in my life."

Luis couldn't argue with that, but he also knew Paolo needed the money to pay the constant stream of care-home bills that were piling up on his coffee table. "Teach me how to do it," he said. "Then maybe you'll get those days off."

Arguing was Paolo's baseline, but for once, he didn't. He shrugged and went back to piling tomatoes onto the kitchen counter. Huge sacks of pasta joined them. Olive oil. Basil. The Italian bacon Luis couldn't pronounce no matter how many times Paolo tried to teach him.

Paolo said something about cheese.

Luis frowned. "What?"

"Mozzarella," Paolo repeated. "I couldn't get enough, so I'm gonna whack some cheddar in. Don't tell Toni."

"I won't."

"Sure about that? You two get on pretty well. If you were a woman, he'd have married us off by now."

"You think he knows we're . . ." Luis couldn't think of a word to describe what he and Paolo were currently doing. Did one even exist for two blokes who worked together by day, played dick tennis at night, but kept almost one hundred per cent of their feelings to their separate selves?

Probably not. Luis settled for a vague hand gesture.

Paolo smirked. "He knows."

"You told him?"

"No. He's just Italian."

Like that explained it. "So he doesn't want to marry you off to a bloke?"

"It's not that. He's just too old and catholic to think outside that particular box. It wouldn't occur to him that queer couples can do all that these days, and I don't have the spoons to explain it to him."

"But he's cool with you being extra-sexual?"

Paolo's smirk morphed into Luis's favourite smile. "If that's what you want to call it, yeah, he's cool. I've never had to worry about shit like that."

The conversation moved on. Paolo taught Luis how to make a huge pot of tomato sauce and layer it with trays and trays of penne pasta. When it was done and stacked up in Paolo's emptied out fridge, they watched Al Pacino films on the couch until they began to doze off.

They went to bed. It was the first night they'd slept together without rolling around for three hours first, but Luis didn't mind. Wrapped around Paolo, listening to him breathe and mutter in his sleep, was almost as good as him being awake.

———

"So, you just stick them in the oven for a bit and that's it?"

Paolo nodded. "That's it. Told you it was easy."

"It's easy today. You spent four hours cooking yesterday, *after* work."

"*We* spent four hours cooking."

"For the first time ever. You're usually on your own."

"Lucky me," Paolo deadpanned around a wide yawn. "Put the salad out and slice the bread if you want to make yourself useful."

Luis did as he was told. When he came back, Paolo was sitting on the kitchen counter, poking at his phone. Luis frowned. At work, Paolo was rarely still, and the trend of being glued to a phone screen seemed to have passed him by. "Everything okay?"

Paolo glanced up with heavy eyes. "Hmm?"

"What's up?"

"Nothing."

"Sure?"

"Of course." Paolo ditched his phone and slid off the counter. "I was just texting Toni back. He's a pain in the arse when Chelsea are playing. Keeps asking me to tape the matches, like anyone still owns a VCR."

"You can't get them on YouTube?"

"Of course. Doesn't stop him asking me to tape them for him. He forgets stuff."

Paolo's eyes darkened again, and Luis realised, not for the first time, that he was out of his depth. He'd never had elderly relatives. His family was small, estranged, and fucked up. He'd never had to worry about the things Paolo worried about, and he'd never hurt the way Paolo did every time the folk who'd raised him faded just a little more.

Luis took the keys from the hook and left the kitchen to open the front door. Unlike weekday mornings, no one was waiting, and previous Sundays had taught him that custom came in lazy trickles rather than mad rushes.

He went back to the kitchen. "Can you take him out?"

"Who?"

"Toni. Is he allowed out of the home?"

"It's not an Institution. He can leave anytime he wants."

"Take him to the pub, then, to watch the Chelsea game."

"I have to work."

"Not if I'm here."

Paolo's face broke into a soft smile, weary at the edges, frayed, but still all kinds of lovely. "You're so fucking sweet."

Luis laughed, couldn't help it. "I'm really not."

"Yeah, you are. No other fucker on earth gives a shit about Toni and his football angst."

"You'll take him then?"

"Maybe next week."

Luis let it go. Paolo was a moody fucker, and despite falling asleep on Luis at ten o'clock the previous night, he seemed tired. Luis made it his mission to give him as little as possible to do, an easy task with the slow custom.

But still, Paolo flagged.

An hour before closing, he came into the kitchen, pale and rubbing his temples. "Man, I feel rough."

Luis ran a tray through the dishwasher. "You look like shit."

"Thanks."

"You want me to lie to you?"

"Keeping your observations to yourself would be better."

Paolo grinned a little, but it looked like a struggle. Luis abandoned the dirty plates and crossed the kitchen to where Paolo was slumped over the counter. He rubbed his back, absorbing the excessive heat beneath Paolo's clothes. "You're hot."

"That's more like it," Paolo said.

"I didn't mean it like that."

"No? Fuck. This shit ain't working."

Behind the obvious signs of fatigue, Paolo looked the same as he always did. A wet dream of olive skin, floppy hair, and perfect bone structure. But he sounded off. Loopy, almost. Unless Luis's hearing had worsened in the last two hours.

He tugged Paolo upright and pulled him into a hug.

Paolo resisted a moment, then sagged against him, moaning softly as Luis massaged the back of his neck. "That's nice."

"Yeah?"

"Yeah. I could fall asleep right here."

Luis would hold him up, but it seemed an uncomfortable place to rest when his flat was a short walk away. "Go home. I'll finish up here."

Paolo shook his head. "I can't ask you to do that again."

"You didn't ask me last time."

"Don't talk circles at me. I can't keep up."

"Then go home. I can do this for you."

Paolo stayed where he was, and for a strung-out moment, Luis feared he'd refuse. Then he let out a sigh that seemed to sap even more of his equilibrium and drew back so Luis could see his face. "You'll be okay? Really?"

Luis pushed Paolo's hair back. "Of course. I'll lock up and bring the cash over when I'm done."

"You're a better man than you think you are."

"You have no idea what I think."

Paolo started to frown, then seemed to change his

mind. He kissed Luis's cheek with dry lips and left. Luis watched him meander across the road, then got to work serving the last few plates of pasta and cleaning down.

It was after five when he left, Paolo's takings tucked into his sock. He was still wearing Paolo's hoodie, but it was beginning to smell more like himself, so he'd have to return it soon. Didn't stop him burying his face in it, though, chasing down what remained of Paolo's scent.

Scent? Fucking wolf now, are you?

For once, the devil on Luis's shoulder made him laugh. He crossed the high street and ducked down the alley that took him to the road behind. Mind on Paolo, he kept his gaze down, paying little attention to the faces he passed. If they weren't Paolo, he didn't give a shit. And despite worrying about him, it felt good to empty his brain of all else. Freeing. As if the soul-deep warmth he felt for Paolo was all he'd ever been meant to feel. That he'd been waiting for him and never known it. Luis wore cynicism like a second skin, but with Paolo, sometimes, he forgot.

I need to be with him.

Two hundred yards, and Luis would get his wish, but as he passed the corner shop, a car pulled up alongside him, rumbling along the kerb until it drew level with Luis, and the window slid open. "Brother."

Luis kept walking. The car followed, then lurched ahead and mounted the pavement. Growling, Luis evaded, but Dante opened the passenger door, blocking his way.

"*Brother*," he repeated, lower this time. Dante never shouted. "Stop being a pussyhole and look at me."

Luis had nowhere to go, unless he wanted to take his

chances in a kerbside brawl. He stopped short of Dante's personal space but kept his gaze fixed on the brick wall behind him. "What do you want?"

"Same thing I wanted the last three times. I want to talk business with you."

"I ain't got no business."

"Course you have. You're my brother."

Not by choice. I'm not your fucking road boy. Luis steeled himself and forced himself to meet Dante's dead-eyed stare.

It swallowed him whole, but not like Paolo's molten gaze. Dante's eyes held no warmth, no humour. Just cold-hearted appraisal as he harvested whatever reaction he'd come looking for. "Look," he tried again. "At least let me give you a ride. Where are you going?"

"Home."

"I know where that is."

"Of course you do. Don't suppose you're gonna tell me how you got my phone number, are you?"

Dante smirked. "I will if you get in the car."

"And if I don't?"

"I'll follow you all the way back to that piece-of-shit bedsit."

Hot fury lanced Luis's gut. In prison, he'd often pictured moments like these, when Dante got up in his face and twisted shit around until Luis didn't know which way was up. In fits of rare optimism, he'd imagined himself driving his knuckles into Dante's smug face, dropping him to the floor, stepping over him, and walking away for good. But reality had always haunted him. He was getting in that car, and Dante knew it.

————

Conversations with Dante had always been a dance across a minefield of unknown width. Every time, Luis trod softly, but still it blew up in his face. And he was out of practice, his senses dulled to Dante's tricks.

"So, you like your job then? Playing straight suits you?"

Luis glowered past the muscle driving for Dante but saw nothing but a hole where his life once was. "I've never played straight."

"Oh, I know. That why you're busting hours in that greasy spoon? For the Italian man candy?"

Luis clenched his fists. *Don't say his fucking name, or I'll kill you, I swear to god.* "It's a job. I need it to pay my rent."

"Crawley Road? Jesus, man. Why do you want to make that skankhole your yard?"

Because it's mine, not yours. Luis shrugged. "I need to stay out of trouble. Prison ain't no joke."

The scar on his head throbbed, but between this meeting, and their first a few weeks back, Dante didn't seem to notice it. He fished a cigarette box from the car door and pulled out a half-smoked joint. "Want some of this?"

Luis rolled his eyes. "You know I don't smoke that shit."

"Maybe you should. Chill you out a bit. You seem tense."

As if Dante knew Luis was wound so tight, every nerve

felt as if it would surely snap. As if he cared. He lit the joint and blew fragrant smoke into Luis's face.

Luis waved it away. "What are you smoking in the car for anyway? You want a stop and search?"

Dante sneered. "For what? A couple of weed buds? Brother, you've been away too long. Police don't care about that shit anymore. They only pull you for the good stuff, and we save that for the fiends."

Luis fought another eye-roll. He used to miss the Dante who didn't talk like he'd eaten the script from a bad TV show, but those days had passed long before Luis had swallowed a six-year stretch. "Whatever. Is there a point to this scenic route home?"

"Does there need to be? You got plans, brother?"

"Nah. I've just got no plans to be here with you."

"Burn."

Luis said nothing. Just breathed in weed smoke and focussed on the roll of notes digging into his ankle. The money Luis was late delivering.

Dante sighed. "You don't make nothing easy."

"I don't have to make anything hard if you'll leave me the fuck alone."

"Can't do that."

"Why not?"

"Cos I need you, my brother."

"Stop calling me that."

"Why? We're blood, man."

"That don't mean shit," Luis exploded. "If we're blood, where the fuck have you been the last six years? And what the fuck have you ever done for me?"

Dante eyed Luis through a haze of smoke. "I done everything for you. Fed you, clothed you, gave you work on the road so you had your own Ps."

Luis laughed. "You put me to work to line your own pocket. Don't be telling it like you were doing me right."

"And don't you be getting emotional. We haven't got time for that. We need to talk business."

"We really don't."

Luis's bedsit, and the last place on earth he wanted to be, came into view. He closed his hand around the door handle.

Dante reached over him and knocked it off. "We do. Unless you want me to keep coming around your work-place, trying to have this conversation again."

Whether he knew it or not, he'd found Luis's weak spot. "You don't need to come to my work. You know where I live."

"Bro, you don't ever sleep in your own bed."

"What do you care about that?"

"Nothing, if you come by the yard tonight and listen properly to what I've got to say. I need your help with something, and it could set you up good. Take you out of that dirt box, man, and into a nice place."

"Oh yeah? And then what? Police knocking at my door? Dragging me back inside? Nah, fam. I'm okay."

"Are you?" Dante leaned closer, and finally his gaze fell on the scar rising up from Luis's skull. "Cos you look like a sad man, innit. And that makes me want to come see you every day, you know? To make sure my baby brother's doing okay."

Luis reclaimed the door handle, but even if he opened it and ran away without looking back, he was trapped. Dante wouldn't give up until he had Luis exactly where he wanted him.

Perhaps he already did.

"What time?"

Dante's lips turned up. "What time what?"

"What time do you want to see me tonight?"

"Any time after ten, bro. I'll be there."

Luis nodded, and right on time, the car eased to a stop by Luis's front door. He got out and shut the door without looking back. The car pulled away and merged with the city traffic. Luis walked slowly towards his front door until he was sure Dante had gone, then spun on his heel and ran in the opposite direction.

He jumped on a bus and rode back to the high street. Paolo's front door appeared in front of him five minutes later. He tapped a light rhythm with his fingertips, and it swung open on the latch.

Luis slipped into Paolo's flat and shut the door behind him with a quiet click. The flat was dark and quiet. Too quiet. Luis toed his shoes off and padded into the living room. Paolo was asleep on the couch, crashed out on his stomach.

His arm was trailing over the side. Luis knelt beside him and took his hand. It was clammy and hot. He squeezed Paolo's fingers, gently at first, then harder when Paolo didn't respond. "Wake up, mate. I brought your money."

Paolo stirred. He cracked his eyes open with a low groan. "Oh. It's you."

"Good job it is. You left your door open."

"Yeah. For you." Paolo pushed himself up. "Fucking hell. What time is it?"

"Seven."

"What?"

"Seven," Luis repeated. "Sorry I'm late. I got held up."

Usually, Paolo missed nothing. Every ounce of bullshit flashed in his dark eyes, even if he didn't say anything. But there was no spark in his gaze now. Just a tired acceptance of Luis's vague half-truth.

He didn't ask for the money.

Luis pulled it from his sock anyway and laid it on the coffee table. Paolo glanced at it but blanched before he could speak and bolted up from the couch.

He left the room and disappeared into the bathroom, slamming the door behind him.

Luis moved to the kitchen to give him some privacy and filled a glass with water. His hands shook, though he couldn't say why. He gazed out of the small window at the city lights twinkling in the darkness. From a tower block, the neighbourhood had always seemed far enough away for him to pretend it was a magical place. From Paolo's window, Luis saw it for what it was—run-down, danger-ous, and all he'd ever known. *Maybe I could leave. Get a job in a different place and be skint and happy there.*

But leaving the city meant leaving Paolo, and—

"You're really here. I was worried I'd hallucinated you."

Luis spun around as Paolo stumbled into the kitchen. "That bad?"

Paolo stepped into Luis's open arms and muttered something into his chest. The words didn't matter. Luis got the sentiment. He hugged Paolo tight and rubbed his back. "You're still burning up. Did you puke before I got here too?"

"A few times. Think I'm over it now, though. I feel better."

"You look like you've died."

"Fucking charmer. Maybe I'll just stay here then and you can move my dead body."

Luis didn't mind. He'd have stood there all night if he thought it would help, but common sense told him Paolo was better off in bed. "Come on. Let's go."

Paolo raised his head. His cheeks were flushed, and yet somehow, his olive skin was deathly pale. "Hmm? What?"

"You're going to bed," Luis said. "Come on."

He looped his arm around Paolo's waist and steered him out of the kitchen. The bedroom was exactly as they'd left it that morning, the side Luis had slept on half made, Paolo's side a riot of rumpled sheets and displaced pillows. Luis's side was furthest away, but putting Paolo in an unmade bed fucked with Luis's head.

Freak. Still. He did it anyway and tried not to ogle as Paolo took his clothes off and flopped back on the bed. Luis knew he should go home, leave Paolo in peace, and deal with his own shit, but even thinking about it hurt his chest.

He leaned over the bed and stroked Paolo's face.

Paolo blinked up at him. "Where you going?"

"Nowhere." Luis toed his shoes off, stripped his T-shirt, and slid under the covers. He held his arm up for Paolo to duck under and rest his head on Luis's chest. "I'm right here."

Paolo knocked out like he'd been drugged. His fever raged on, but in the early hours of the morning, his shallow breaths evened out, and his skin cooled.

Relieved, Luis took a deep breath of his own and slipped out of bed. He'd left his phone in the living room. It was flashing on the coffee table with a message.

Unknown number: *uve fucked me off too many times now bro. real talk comin*

13

Paolo woke to cool hands on his face and soft lips on his cheek.

"Go back to sleep," Luis whispered. "I'll open the cafe."

It was too good to be true. Paolo struggled to sit up, but Luis pushed him back, and the jackhammer still raging in Paolo's head took his side. *I don't want you to go.*

But Luis left anyway, and when Paolo next woke, it was light outside. His headache had faded to a dull roar. The nausea was gone, and he no longer felt like he was burning a forest fire under his skin.

He sat up, squinting against the single ray of winter sunshine bursting through a gap in the curtains. His phone was on the bedside table with an empty bottle of water and a box of paracetamol with four broken tabs. Paolo frowned. He didn't remember drinking anything or swallowing any pills, but then, all he could truly recall was throwing his guts up a hundred times before Luis had appeared in the living room like an apparition. Even stumbling to bed was a haze of warmth and strong arms. *God, I hope I didn't puke on him.*

As the thought crossed his mind, his phone buzzed. Paolo reached for it and opened the flurry of messages Toni had sent about Match of the Day the previous night.

Paolo: *didn't watch it, threw up all night instead*

Toni: *r u ok?*

Paolo: *totally fine, but can't visit tonight, home rules, remember?*

Toni: *i remember not lost my marbles yet boy dont visit Carmela either*

Paolo: *I won't*

No reply came. Head spinning from Toni's aversion to punctuation, Paolo dropped his phone on the bed and closed his eyes. Despite sleeping most of the last twenty-four hours, he started to drift and jumped a mile when his phone buzzed again.

Toni: *can luis come instead*

Paolo: *are u serious?*

Toni: *why not he doesn't move my things around I like him*

It was as good a reason as any, Paolo supposed, but

Luis had done him enough favours to last a lifetime. There was no way he was asking him to spend his evening visiting an old folks' home. It was bad enough that he was running the cafe alone for minimum wage. *And you still haven't paid his rent, remember?* It wasn't due yet, but Paolo knew Luis was antsy about it. He'd left the paperwork in the kitchen a few days ago.

Ignoring the lingering headache, Paolo swung his legs out of bed and trudged to the shower. The hot spray made him feel less grungy, and the blast of cold water when it ran out woke him up enough for him to put himself together and leave the flat.

He took Luis's housing card to the post office and paid his rent. Then he stopped by the corner shop and bought electricity tokens. Luis hadn't mentioned running short, but he rarely mentioned much unless Paolo dragged it out of him.

The sun was still shining as he walked to the cafe. Shoppers bustled around, buying produce from the market, and dickhead lads in their shit cars cruised up and down the high street, blaring bad music and honking of weed smoke. A black car burned past and mounted the pavement in front of Paolo. Scowling, he stepped around it and continued on his way. *Wankers.*

At the cafe, he found Luis running the show with flaw-less efficiency. Bacon and sausages sizzled on the grill while he cleared tables and took orders at the till. Somehow he managed it without uttering more than two words to anyone, but that was Luis. Quietly beautiful.

Paolo came up behind him at the grill and laid a soft

hand on his back, the warning he'd learned to use to let Luis know he was there. "I could go on holiday for a month and come back to find you run this place better than me."

Luis snorted. "Be my guest. Just keep me away from the paperwork."

"Speaking of which." Paolo handed over Luis's payment card and the receipt for his rent, along with electricity tokens. "I didn't know if you needed these, but I got them anyway. You'll need them eventually, right?"

"You didn't need to do that today. You should be in bed."

"Fuck off. It's shit without you. And I'm fine now. Whatever it was has gone away."

Luis treated Paolo to a searching stare that made him feel stark naked in front of every cafe patron lost in their all-day breakfast. "Are you sure? Cos you said that last night and you were lying."

"Mistaken. I'd never lie to you."

"Wouldn't you?"

"No."

Luis never wasted words. He nodded and turned back to the grill. Paolo shook his head and marvelled at how a conversation could become so deep so fast. How Luis could flay him open with a simple question. He wanted to rip the tongs from Luis's hands and shake him. Make him believe that he was worth so much more than how his arsehole family had treated him. But Paolo never wanted to *make* Luis do anything. If he was ever going to have a little faith, he'd have to find it himself.

Paolo ditched his coat in the kitchen and retreated to

the fridge to make a list for the wholesale order. The cool air made him shiver, but after a night of sweltering in his own skin, he welcomed it. His headache ran its course, and by the time Luis brought his vibrating phone to him, he felt halfway human.

"Someone really wants to talk to you," Luis said.

He started to leave, but Paolo didn't feel like letting him go so fast. He grabbed his hand and yanked him back in.

Luis let him and crowded Paolo against the racks of produce stacked on the shelves. "You really are feeling better?"

"I am. I meant it when I said I'd never lie to you."

Luis dipped his head for a kiss. Their lips met in a sweet collision, and suddenly all was right with the world. Paolo slid his hands under Luis's T-shirt and ghosted his palms over warm skin that went on for days. Heat pooled where he wanted Luis most, but short of dropping his jeans in the fridge, there wasn't much he could do about that.

His phone was still buzzing. Irritated, he pulled back and glowered at the screen. "Jesus fucking Christ."

Luis buried his face in Paolo's neck and kissed a path to Paolo's collarbone. "Something wrong?"

Paolo swayed on his feet, tipped upside down by Luis's attention to his throat. "Not unless you count Toni driving me insane."

"What's he doing?"

"Celebrating that I can't go and see him tonight. Apparently, I mess with his stuff too much."

"Why can't you go?"

"Because I've been sick. I have to leave it forty-eight hours before I go back. Home policy to protect the residents."

"Makes sense."

"I know, I just hate leaving him by himself. Nonna's okay when she's with it enough to know where she is. She's made friends. Toni's not like that. He hates other people."

"How did he run this place for so long then?"

"Same as me. By shouting at everyone."

"You don't shout."

"You can't hear me half the time, which is probably just as well. I annoy myself most days."

Luis laughed. "I told you already, everything annoys you."

"You don't. And apparently, you don't annoy Toni either. He's bugging me because he wants you to visit him instead. Just tonight, I think, but maybe forever. He wasn't specific."

"He wants me to visit him?"

"Yeah, but don't worry. I've already told him no."

"Why?"

"Because my grandparents aren't your problem."

"No, I meant why does he want to see me? Have I done something wrong?"

"What? Why would you think that?"

Luis shrugged. "Dunno. Why else would he want me to visit?"

"Because he likes you, Luis."

"Wow. You never say my name."

"Don't I?

"No. But I like it when you do. It sounds nice."

"You say the strangest things."

"Not on purpose."

"I know." Paolo kissed Luis again and forgot that they were in the fridge. Forgot everything except how Luis's lips felt against his. How his warm body melded to his own as if they'd been made to fit together in a perfect puzzle. Only more insistent buzzing from his phone drove them apart.

Luis laughed. "Toni again?"

"I'm ignoring him." Paolo dropped his phone in his pocket.

"Why?"

"Because he's only messaging me to wind me up. I already told him no."

"Why did you tell him no when you hadn't asked me?"

"Because I have zero intention of asking you."

Luis took Paolo's hand and towed him out of the fridge. Back in the warmth, he lifted Paolo as if he weighed nothing and deposited him on the counter.

Paolo laughed too. "Dick. Don't manhandle me."

"Why? It's the same as you answering that question without asking me."

"It's really not."

"It really is. Why is it okay for you to tell your granddad I won't come and see him when you haven't even asked me?"

"Dude, it's not your responsibility."

"It doesn't need to be if I want to do it. It can just be fun."

"Your idea of fun is hanging around an old folks'

home? Jesus, you're not right in the head. I hate those places."

"You wouldn't have liked prison either, then."

"Did you?"

Luis's gaze turned thoughtful and then so distant that Paolo shook him gently to bring him back. "It's a complicated question," Luis said. "Of course I hated it, but being outside isn't that different sometimes."

"In what sense?"

"Nothing specific. I just don't feel all that free."

Paolo was missing something. He knew it like he knew water was wet, but figuring it out scared him. He liked the bubble they'd created around themselves. The cocoon of days and nights where Luis's secrets didn't matter. He used his legs to draw Luis in, then wrapped his arms around him in the tight hug Luis had needed the very first day he'd walked into the cafe. "I'm sorry you don't feel free."

———

Luis visited Toni every night for a week while Paolo caught up on sleep, the accounts, and everything else he'd let slide. He cooked dinner, washed the bedsheets, and played FIFA for the first time in months. It was like a holiday, and Luis was the sunshine.

"I think you got sick because you've been doing too much," Luis mused one night. "If it was a bug, I'd have got it too." He had his eyes closed while Paolo was tracing pictures on his bare skin. It was late and they'd have to sleep soon, but Paolo didn't want to. He wanted to stay awake like this, with Luis, forever.

He laid his head on Luis's chest. "Maybe. I'm glad you didn't, though. But you know I would've taken care of you if you had, don't you? Like you've taken care of me?"

"I didn't do anything."

"Whatever." Paolo wasn't going to debate that point again. Luis wasn't good at being told he mattered, and Paolo didn't know how to fix it. He lay still a moment, listening to Luis's heartbeat against his cheek, a steady metronome that fought the chaos he so often saw in Luis's eyes. He'd seen it today, in the supermarket that was a world away from the corner store Luis usually shopped at.

"I can't choose. There's too many."

"Don't choose then." Paolo snagged a tin of tomatoes from the shelf. "Just take the nearest one. And I don't know why you're buying these anyway. I literally have a thousand kilos of them at home."

Luis's frown had deepened, and he'd walked away without the tomatoes, leaving Paolo bemused. It had taken him a while to figure out giving Luis everything he needed was as suffocating as taking it away.

Paolo sat up. "Can I ask you something?"

Luis cracked a wary eye open. "Okay."

"You can say no if you want, even before you know what it is."

"I didn't say no."

"I know, I'm just saying— You know what? Never mind."

Paolo lay back down. Luis nudged him until he looked

at him again. "Just ask me the question. What kind of arse-hole do you think I am?"

"I don't think you're an arsehole."

Luis made a gesture that was as impatient as he ever seemed to get.

Paolo took the hint. "What's it like being outside after so long in prison? Most days, I forget about it, then random shit seems to freak you out, and I wondered if they were connected."

Luis sighed. "Are you talking about the tomato thing again?"

"And the park thing."

"What park thing?"

"You didn't like it when we walked home through the park the other day. It was like you'd never seen the sky."

"It's a big park."

"So?"

"I haven't been in open space like that for a while."

Paolo crawled up Luis's body and kissed him, throwing a leg over his waist for good measure. With Luis's dick hard beneath him, it was easy to forget they were having a serious conversation. Too easy. But, fuck, if he couldn't stop kissing Luis. They'd already fooled around on the couch, making each other groan and come while the evening news droned in the background. Sometimes Paolo worried Luis would suck him dry. Then they'd kiss, and his body would come to life like the first time all over again. But . . . this wasn't the time. He'd opened a can of worms, and he needed to put the lid back on.

He broke the kiss and pressed his forehead against

Luis's. "Sorry. I keep making you explain stuff that should be obvious to me. I never knew I was this fucking dense."

"You're not dense. And it's stupid anyway, at least the tomato thing was. It's not like there weren't a thousand different types before I went down. It was six years ago, not sixty. I had two iPhones and a car with its own sat nav. It's not like I didn't know how the world worked."

"What happened to it?"

"What? The car?"

"Yeah."

"It was confiscated as proceeds of crime, even though I bought it with the money my dad left me."

"Can't you get it back?"

"I don't care enough to find out."

"Did you lose anything else? Apart from the obvious, I mean."

Luis shook his head. "Only cash and tools that scare the shit out of me now."

"Tools? You mean, like weapons?"

"Why do you want to know this stuff?"

Paolo didn't. He'd stopped equating the Luis who shared his bed with the feared road boy he'd once been. But the masochist in him wouldn't quit. Or maybe it was the nosy old woman Nonna had once told him he'd been born to be. "I just want to be there for you as much as you've been there for me, and that's hard when I don't really know you."

"You don't need to know the police found two zombie knives and a samurai sword under my bed to know who I am now."

While they'd talked, Luis's gaze had drifted back to the ceiling. Paolo felt like gripping his chin and forcing him to look at him, but he didn't want to be that person in Luis's life. Fuck, in anyone's life. "I want to know what you did."

"When?"

"When you went to prison. Toni knows, but he won't tell me."

"How come you don't know?"

"I don't read the local papers or watch the news."

"We literally just watched the news."

"If you were watching the news, I need to suck your dick better."

"I'd combust if you sucked my dick any better."

Paolo loved how Luis talked about sex, deadpan and yet so fucking filthy. And he understood the sentiment. Luis's wicked mouth blew his mind *and* his cock. He didn't care for the deflection, though. Was it so hard for Luis to tell him to mind his own business?

Then again, perhaps Google would've been easier than making Luis relive whatever had landed him a six-year stretch.

Paolo laid his head down again, assuming the conversation was over.

Luis slid his hands into Paolo's hair and tugged him back up. "It was armed robbery in the end, and a GBH charge that should've been worse."

"GBH?"

"Yeah. The CPS wanted attempted murder, but the dude we hurt shouldn't have been there, so they couldn't prove that we had a premeditated plan to kill him."

"You killed someone?"

"No! God no. But we could've done. And that's why I think I should've got the worse charge."

"You said 'we.' Who else was there?"

"It doesn't matter."

It didn't. Luis was all Paolo cared about, but the burning need to know everything made Paolo's skin itch. "What happened? Weren't you making enough money in the tower blocks?"

"Of course we were making enough. But what happens to people when they have more money than sense?"

"They don't all nearly kill someone."

"But they all get greedy. And they start to believe what other people say about them. You hear yourself called a king enough times, eventually, you think it's true."

"I can't imagine you ever thinking like that."

"I didn't say it was me."

Dante. Of course. It had to be.

As if he'd heard the penny drop in Paolo's mind, Luis sat up, dislodging Paolo from his chest. He swung his legs out of bed and stood, then sat down again, for once, wearing his emotions like Paolo did. "It was fucking stupid, and I told him it was never going to work. That we weren't cut out to be hustlers like that, but he didn't listen. He'd got cosy with some crew in Liverpool, and they'd made him feel like a big man. It didn't matter what I said. It was happening."

"Who did you rob?"

"Attempt to rob. We fucked it up, remember?"

GARRETT LEIGH

Paolo's hand hovered over Luis's rigid shoulders, but he bottled it and let it drop. "You don't have to tell me."

"I know. You've said that already, but . . . I want to. I want you to know who's visiting your grandparents and sharing your bed at night."

"So tell me who you were back then. It doesn't have to be who you are now."

"Doesn't it?"

"No. Six years is a long time."

"I don't need you to tell me that."

Of course he didn't. He didn't need any of this. He needed a good night's sleep after working all day for minimum wage, then spending his evening listening to Toni lecture him on how to make perfect cannoli. He didn't need a trip down memory lane that made him look like he was about to throw up.

But here they were.

Luis leaned forward, elbows on his knees. "We held up a Securitas van, you know the ones that transport cash? Dante thought we'd get away with sixty grand, but it wasn't even about the money for him. He was trying to be a fucking gangster, a real one, not a council estate slinger."

Dante Pope was gangster enough for Paolo, but he said nothing. Just rubbed Luis's back, hoping he'd continue.

"Anyway," Luis said, "he had this stupid plan to steal a flatbed lorry to ram the van off the road and a fucking tractor—can you believe it?—to get it from behind."

"A tractor?"

"I know. Trust me, I still don't get the logic behind that."

"Did it work?"

"Yeah, to start with. We smashed the back doors in and got to the money."

"Then what?"

"We ran to the other car. If we'd got in and driven off, we might've got away with it, or at least without anyone getting hurt, but Dante wanted more, so we went back."

Luis's tone was matter of fact, as if he was reading from a newspaper article about traffic congestion, but his shoulders remained locked, and tiny shivers that Paolo might not have noticed if he wasn't touching him shuddered beneath his skin.

"What happened when you went back?"

Luis twisted his hands so tight Paolo feared he'd snap his fingers off. "The driver had got out—he thought we'd gone. And he had someone with him too, a driver's mate we hadn't accounted for. He was round the back, assessing the damage. We didn't see him until we were on top of him, and by then, it was too late. He'd used his phone to take pictures of us, and he wouldn't give it up without a fight."

Paolo sucked in a quiet breath. "Did you even get the phone from him?"

"Yeah, but it didn't matter in the end."

"Why not?"

"Because it was me who gave it to the police."

Paolo sat back against the headboard, mourning the loss of Luis's overheated skin against his palm but needing the space for his brain to catch up. "I don't understand."

"Some days, neither do I. I've had to train myself not to

think about it or I go too deep, man, and I can't come back."

"You're here now."

"I know." Luis turned to face Paolo. "And that's why I have to tell you everything. I can't tell half this story anymore. It fucking kills me, you know? It's like when you open a fizzy bottle when it's been shaken up. You twist the cap and your fingers get wet, and you have to take it all the way off to make it stop."

It made sense, but the analogy didn't sound like a conclusion Luis would've come to on his own. *Counselling, perhaps? Do they even do that in prison?* Shamefully, Paolo had no idea. "Tell me what happened."

Luis shrugged. "Dante's a shit fighter, always has been. People are scared of him because he's manipulated them into thinking he does his own dirty work. But he doesn't; he's got a payroll full of muscle for that now."

"And before? It was you, right?"

"Some of it. I hadn't done anyone serious damage until that day, though, because he'd never been there to make me. But this dude . . . fuck, he didn't want to give that phone up. I fought him hard, and I might've won, but Dante threw me a crowbar and told me to hit the dude with it."

"Then what?"

"I did what I was told."

"Why?"

"Because I was twenty-one and as sucked into my brother's rep as everyone else? Because I was a piece-of-shit mash man who didn't care that I could've killed a dude just doing his job? I don't fucking know." Luis wrapped his arms around himself and rocked back and forth. His eyes were damp, but no tears fell. "Dante ran away. He was screaming at me to follow him, but when I looked down and saw the blood by my feet, I couldn't move. I fell over— I don't know if I fainted or just lost my fucking mind—but Dante didn't come back for me. He got in the car and left me there, and I didn't even care."

Paolo had stopped breathing. His head pounded, and his cheeks felt numb. He let out a shuddery breath. "I can't believe he left you."

Luis hissed through his teeth. "I can. And I'm glad he did. I stayed with the Securitas men and tried to stop the man I'd hit from dying. When the police came, I gave them the phone, and told them the man with the red mask was me."

"You never told them who Dante was?"

"No."

"Why not?"

Luis finally lifted his red-eyed gaze to meet Paolo's. "Because he doesn't deserve redemption."

14

It took Luis a week to figure out Dante had got his phone number from the teenage girl who worked in the bank, the one who wouldn't unlock his account without photo ID. He'd asked her three times. Begged her. Then he'd just so happened to be outside the bank when it had closed, and she'd left. A blacked-out car had picked her up and driven her towards the Moss Farm tower blocks and guided her towards Luis's childhood home. *Good for you, sweetheart. He won't be banging you for long.*

Or maybe he would. Maybe nothing had changed about Dante except his propensity for treating women like shit. Perhaps he'd marry this one.

"What are you raging about?"

"Hmm?" Luis refocussed. Paolo was beside him, face caught between a frown and a glare. "Sorry, what?"

"You look really pissed off."

"Find a mirror, dude."

Paolo's scowl deepened. "I'd rather find the order slip

for table four. She reckons she's been waiting half an hour for beans on toast."

"You don't do beans on toast."

"*We* don't do beans on toast. I don't remember anything that happened in my life before you."

"That's sweet."

Paolo huffed. "If you say so. Where's that fucking order?"

Luis didn't have it. Since Paolo had been ill, he'd forced himself back to the grill, and he kept every slip of paper Paolo passed him in a bulldog clip by the bacon. The beans on toast order wasn't there. "Do you want me to cook it anyway?"

"Fuck no," Paolo snapped. "She didn't bloody order it, and we don't even have beans, remember?"

He stomped away, leaving Luis to marvel at how someone so bad tempered could make him feel so damn good. But the further Paolo was away from him, the quicker his humour faded. His thoughts returned to Dante and the barrage of messages he'd sent since Luis had stood him up. They'd all come from different numbers, but even though he'd dropped the "bro" bullshit, Luis knew it was him.

Who else would warn him it was only a matter of time before the "pretty boy" in his life found out who he really was?

Luis didn't want to think about what Dante would do if he found out Paolo already knew. That Luis had told him everything about that fateful day and more.

Paolo came back with the order slip he'd found by

the till. Luis took it without gloating and cooked the plate of tomatoes on toast it had been amended to. Paolo didn't appear to collect it straight away. Sighing, Luis picked it up and turned around, facing the cafe for the first time since it had opened. Table four was at the back. It was occupied by the girl from the bank, and she wasn't alone.

———

Fury darkened Luis's vision. He gripped the plate so hard it tipped sideways, sloshing hot, olive oil slick tomatoes over his hand.

He barely felt it. In his head, he crossed the cafe, throat punched Dante, and hurled him out onto the street, but in reality, he didn't move. Couldn't. It was the third time he'd faced his brother since he'd got out, but seeing him here, in *Paolo's* cafe, chilled him to the bone.

Paolo was at the next table, clearing it onto a huge tray. He hadn't noticed Dante yet, but other people had. How long before they saw Luis too? Dante wouldn't be ignored, and what then? Paolo had told him a dozen times he couldn't have Luis's bullshit in the cafe. What if he told Dante too?

Dante's reputation was scary as fuck, but Luis knew Paolo well enough to know he wouldn't give a shit if Dante wound him up. Which Dante would, because he was a manipulative motherfucker who'd always known Luis's weak spots.

And there was no doubt that Paolo was Luis's weak

spot now. He didn't care about his job, his crappy flat, his freedom. Nothing mattered more than Paolo.

Fuck. I love him.

The realisation nearly sent Luis to his knees. Only Dante's presence kept him upright. He set the plate down, wiped it clean with a paper towel, and rinsed his hands. His skin was an angry pink where the oil had burned him, and the stinging pain merged with the rage building inside.

He took the plate to the table and dumped it in front of Dante's girl. "What do you want?"

Dante's grin widened. "Chicken sandwich. Mayo, no salad."

Of course he did. That bland shit was all he ever ate. Luis bit back a sneer. "Don't do them here. Read the fucking menu."

He walked away, blood roaring in his ears, skin hot with the worst kind of heat. Instinct urged him into the kitchen and away from Dante, but that meant leaving Paolo alone with him, and Luis couldn't do it. Not now, not ever.

More orders came in. Luis cooked without seeing the food he was putting on plates. Dante's presence behind him burned every moment he was there, and Luis knew the second he wasn't.

Tension flooded out of him with a dizzying sigh. He leant on the worktop and hung his head, ignoring the frantic sizzle of the bacon he was about to char to an inedible crisp *Bastard, bastard, bastard.* He'd known it was coming but had clung to the hope that he'd had more time. That Dante would give him a little longer with Paolo before he took it all away.

Cos that's what he did—what he'd always done. Given Luis enough rope to think he was free, then yanked on it so hard he broke everything Luis had ever touched. They'd told him in prison that Dante's hold on him was psychological abuse. Even then, Luis hadn't truly understood it, but he did now.

Paolo came up behind him, his hand first on Luis's back, then his lips at Luis's good ear. "He's gone."

Despite the warning, Luis jumped a mile. "Who?"

"Don't give me that. I saw you talking to him."

"I didn't talk to him."

"Are you okay?"

A week ago, Luis could've shrugged the question off, but ever since the night Luis had purged his soul, it had felt like Paolo saw every emotion that passed through him. He shook his head. "I wish he was dead."

"Do you? Or is it the fact that you still love him that twists you up so much?"

"I don't love him."

"It's okay if you do."

"I don't."

Paolo sighed. "Sorry. That sounded super patronising anyway, so feel free to punch me in the face."

The only thing Luis wanted to do to Paolo right then didn't involve an audience of people eating the Italian sausages Paolo had put on the specials board. He shook his head again, the heat of the grill suddenly so fierce he couldn't stand it. "Can I go out?"

"What?"

"Out. I need to go out."

"Of course." Paolo stood back to let him pass. "Take as long as you—"

Luis didn't hear him. He took his apron off, dropped it on the floor, and fled the cafe. Outside, the cold winter breeze did nothing to calm him, and he took off at a run with no real clue where he was going. The high street passed him by, then the new build flats where Paolo lived, and the grubby alleyways he still knew like the back of his hand. The shopping complex at the base of the tower block he'd once called home, and the grimy stairs that led to the very top floor.

Muscle lined the stairwells of the uppermost floors. Perhaps they'd have stopped anyone else, but Luis breezed on by until he got to the top. There two faces he recognised were waiting for him, blocking his path.

Luis stepped up to them. "I need to see my brother."

Asa, the biggest, meanest dude on Dante's payroll unless you knew him the way Luis did, shook his head. "He ain't seeing anyone."

"Give a fuck. He'll see me."

"Nah, Luis. He told us you'd come and not to let you in."

Asa and Luis had once been as close to friends as any boys on the road could get, closer, even, but Luis had been gone a long time, and Asa had moved up in the world.

Luis turned to the other one, Martell. Dante's man through and through, he was easier to read. "You know

Dante. He said he don't want to see me cos he wants you to go tell him I'm asking. You know how he be."

If anyone did better than Luis, it was Martell. He rolled his eyes and pulled his phone from his jacket pocket. "Wait here."

Luis leaned against the grubby wall that had once been white. Martell disappeared. Asa stared straight ahead, ignoring Luis entirely, and Luis didn't care enough to make him do anything else. Besides, Dante wouldn't keep him waiting long. It wasn't his style.

True to form, Martell reappeared ten minutes later and waved Luis through. "He told me to tell you to take your shoes off."

"Fuck you." Luis stuck his finger up and pushed past. The corridor was lined with more heavies, but none looked at him as he made his way to the door at the end. It was open. Luis slipped inside and shut it behind him. Instinct told him Dante was alone; he'd never liked having people in his yard, even his homeboys.

White carpet lined the hallway. Luis kept his shoes on and kicked doors open until he found Dante in the living room, dressed up in his best designer boxers to watch his gigantic TV by himself. He smirked from his shiny leather couch. "Miss me already, brother?"

"Don't call me that."

"Really? Again? You can't deny blood. However much you want to."

"You have no idea how much I want to."

"No? So why don't you tell me?"

"Why don't you leave me the fuck alone?"

Dante reached for a blunt on the coffee table. He lit up without offering it to Luis and blew a haze of herbal smoke into the air. "I already told you. We need to talk business."

"We haven't got any business."

"Of course we have. We're brothers."

"Stop saying that."

Dante rolled his eyes. "If you've come here to talk in circles, don't bother. I ain't here for that. Go back to your greasy spoon and wait for me there. I know where to find you."

I know where to find you. It was Dante's favourite phrase, and it had haunted Luis his whole fucking life. He heard it in his worst dreams. "Don't come to my work again."

"Why not? It's a free country, and your boy toy didn't seem to mind me being there."

Luis fought the reaction Dante was obviously looking for. There was still a chance he didn't know for sure that it was Paolo's bed he'd been sharing when he hadn't been home. That he was testing Luis to see if he'd break. And fuck, Luis wanted to break. He wanted to break every bone in Dante's body and leave him to rot on his chavtastic sofa. "He didn't know who you were cos he doesn't care. He's not interested in my personal life."

"That right? So why is he paying your rent for you?"

"He's not."

"Yes he is. He was in the post office yesterday with your rent card, paying your bills like he's your fucking wife or some shit."

"He did that for me because I don't have a bank account. It was my money."

Dante grinned. "You do have a bank account. Why else would you go into the bank three times and ask them to unlock it?"

"They didn't do it yet. Bae's probably too busy with your dick down her throat."

"Probably. Maybe I should ask her to take better care of you. Or I could get her to suck your dick, if you're still into women, that is. Prison can fuck with a man like that."

"I didn't need prison to know I like all kinds of folk to suck my dick."

"That's cute, brother. But don't be saying that shit on the street. I haven't got time to protect you from that."

"From what? What homeboy on the street cares who's sucking my dick?"

Dante stubbed his smoke out in a nearby ashtray. "None of them until I direct them to that cosy cafe of yours—"

Luis blurred across the room and yanked Dante off the sofa by his neck. He threw him against the wall, blind rage stoked by the flash of shock in Dante's eyes. "Stay away from the cafe."

Dante tried to speak.

Luis pressed his forearm over his throat. "I mean it, stay the fuck away. I don't need your bullshit in my face when I'm trying to work."

Dante's face reddened, and his eyes bulged. He scrabbled for his phone in his pocket, but Luis got there first and tossed it aside. He pushed harder against Dante's windpipe, and a red mist descended. *You could kill him. Be free of him forever.* But Luis was no longer a slave to the madness that made him want his brother dead. He was a man who wanted to grill bacon all day and hold Paolo all night long, not spend the rest of his life looking over his shoulder in prison.

He let Dante go.

Dante slumped against the wall, rubbing his neck. "You know I could have you whacked right here right now, don't you? For that shit you just pulled?"

"Go on then. I don't care."

"You really don't, do you? About yourself. It's that cafe boy that's got you worried."

Luis couldn't deny it. What was the point? He'd given himself away the moment he'd thrown hands. "What do you *want*?"

Dante stopped rubbing his neck and returned to the couch to relight his blunt. His first drag made him cough, and he rubbed his neck again. "I was going to ask you to do me some muscle work, but seeing as you've got yourself some anger issues, I don't want you on the street like that. Reckon you'd make a better mule."

"What?"

"You heard me, bruh. I got food I need moving up north. I want you to take it."

Food. Man, it had been a long time since Luis had heard the street slang for the kilos and kilos of coke and smack Dante moved around the city. Prison had a language all of its own. "What do you mean, up north? You got some county lines shit up and running?"

"County what? Don't be saying that up in here. Just take the food where I tell you."

"I ain't doing shit for you."

Dante rolled his shoulders in an easy shrug. "That's your choice, but I've already told you what's gonna happen if you don't."

"Why me? Why can't you use some wide boy who actually wants this life?"

"I don't need wide boys. I need you. My brother. Cos I know you're good for keeping your mouth shut."

"That's not true. I took a six-year stretch because I pled guilty. I didn't keep my mouth shut about anything."

"You never said shit about me. You took them years for your family."

"I took them for myself." The truth hit Luis like a sucker punch. As if saying it out loud had solidified it enough to be real. "I took them to get away from you."

Dante laughed. "How's that working out for you, considering you're in my flat?"

It wasn't Dante's flat. It belonged to the council, just as it had twenty years ago when it had been their family home. Luis couldn't believe Dante still had it. How many strings had he pulled to keep the tenancy? Or maybe it was still in their mother's name. Whatever. Luis didn't give a fuck. He only cared about Paolo.

He stepped up to Dante again and leaned over him. "You gotta leave him alone."

"Who?"

"You know who."

"Do I?"

Luis fought the urge to grab Dante by the neck again

and squeeze him until his smug face turned blue. "Yeah. You do. What the fuck do you want from me?"

"I already told you. I need you to move some food."

"Why? Have you run out of grunts you can trust?"

Dante's eyes flashed, and Luis knew he'd hit the jackpot. But it didn't matter. As long as Dante believed Paolo to be Luis's most precious thing, he'd dig his claws in until Luis gave up what he wanted most—control. *Maybe you can do one job for him. Fuck it up so he doesn't ask you again.* But it would never be that simple. Fucking up meant violence or prison or both, and life with Paolo had rendered Luis unequipped for either. He had a job now and a man he'd die to protect, even if he had to go back on the road to do it.

Don't. If you give in now, it'll never stop.

But neither would Dante. Paolo was as tough as any road man Luis had ever known, but he didn't deserve the fire Dante would light beneath them if he didn't get his way.

Sensing victory in Luis's silence, Dante clapped a cold hand on Luis's shoulder. "I've got some shit to figure out before I need you. Wait for my contact, then show up when and where I tell you to."

"And if I don't?"

Dante leered. "Then I'll burn your world down, brother."

15

Luis didn't come back to work. Paolo closed up alone and left. Sometimes, on Luis's rare days off, Paolo would find him in the shadows outside his building, clutching a bag of tricks to make them both dinner. But there was no one waiting for Paolo when he got home. Just an empty flat and a rumpled bed.

He kicked around for a while, tidying the things Luis usually did—the bed, the couch, the towels on the bathroom floor. But without Luis, the stillness of the quiet flat got under his skin. He caved and sent Luis a message.

Paolo: *going to see Toni in a bit. want me to leave you a key?*

Luis: *can't, got to do something*

Paolo: *k, want dinner later?*

Luis didn't reply, and he hated talking on the phone enough for Paolo to think twice about calling him. *Idiot. Even if he doesn't answer, at least he'll know you called.*

And then what? If Luis had gone to see Dante, the last thing he needed was Paolo blowing up his phone.

The daylight faded. It was dark by the time Paolo admitted defeat and left the flat alone, and the bus ride to see Toni wasn't quite long enough to zone out from how much he missed Luis, despite the fact they'd been together a few hours ago.

He signed into the care home. Toni was in the rec room at the back, pretending to play solitaire so he didn't have to talk to anyone, a strange concept for a man who had plenty to say.

Paolo nodded from the doorway. "You want me to come in, or you wanna take a walk?"

"Come here, boy. That programme about the island is on in a minute."

"What island?"

"The one where the giant lizards live."

Paolo threaded around the clusters of old folk sleeping, watching TV, or hosting visitors of their own, and joined Toni at his favourite armchair. He found a stool and sunk onto it. Long days were nothing new, but it was hard to believe he had an entire evening to get through before he could go to bed. He didn't want to think about how he'd feel if Luis wasn't there.

Why wouldn't he be there? He's always there.

Always. Yeah, right. How had a few weeks of companionship turned into a normal Paolo couldn't give up?

"What's the matter with you?" Toni grumbled. "And where's Luis? He owes me a quid from yesterday's game."

"What game?"

"The Arsenal game."

"You don't follow Arsenal."

"Luis said they'd win. I said they wouldn't, so he owes me a quid."

"He doesn't even like football."

"No, but his dad did."

It bothered Paolo that Toni knew that and he didn't. They'd had so many heavy conversations recently, the small stuff, like learning what the other liked, outside of epic blowjobs, had fallen by the wayside. "Fine. I'll tell him when I see him."

"When will that be?"

"Tomorrow. At work."

"He's not staying over?"

"No. He doesn't do that every night."

"Why not?"

"Why would he?"

Toni gave Paolo the kind of look that would've been better coming from Nonna. "I thought you two were courting?"

"What? When have I ever *courted* anyone? Have you regressed to your childhood?"

"I don't know what else you would call it, boy. He didn't talk about you like someone you'd meet on that sex app on your phone."

"Grindr isn't a sex app," Paolo lied for the millionth time. "And I don't have it on my phone anymore."

"Because you're courting Luis?"

"Because I don't use it anymore."

"Because you're—"

"Stop saying that." Paolo reached for a biscuit and pretended to shove it in Toni's mouth to shut him up. "I don't know if Luis is staying over tonight, okay? He left work early."

"Why?"

"I don't know. He might've gone to see his brother."

Toni sobered. The playfulness in his old eyes dulled. "His brother? He told me he didn't want anything to do with him."

"I don't think he does, but Dante came looking for him today."

"Where?"

"At the cafe."

"Oh." Toni sat back in his chair. "That's not good."

Paolo sighed. "I was hoping you'd think it was nothing to worry about."

"Of course it's something to worry about. That brother is scum. We don't want his kind in our place or around Luis."

"We don't get to pick his family for him."

"But he should. He doesn't want this, you know that. He just wants a quiet life."

"He won't get that with us."

"You know what I mean. He's not built for the life he's led, no?"

Paolo couldn't argue with that. Luis's tale of what had gone down to land him in prison had shaken Paolo to the core, but his shock had nothing on the trauma he'd seen pass through Luis's eyes as he'd told his story. And what about the scar on his head? Retaliation, he'd said, that had landed him with enough damage to ruin his hearing. But what about the scars Paolo couldn't see? His own life had been tough, but he'd got through it with the love and support he'd had at home. Luis had never had that. His father was dead, his mother gone, and his brother was an evil piece of shit who used him for his own gain.

Whatever Luis had done in the lifetime he'd lived before he'd walked into Toni's cafe, he deserved better. "He told me what he did," Paolo said, breaking the brooding silence that had stretched out between him and Toni. "About the Securitas van and the man he hurt. I was pissed off with you when you wouldn't tell me before, but I'm glad you didn't."

"Why?"

"Because I'm a self-centred dickbag who needed to get to know him before I was ready to deal with that shit."

"I don't know this dickbag insult you throw at yourself, boy. But if there's one thing you're not, it's self-centred. If you were, you'd still have that app on your phone, and you wouldn't be here, spending your evening with your old nonno."

"If you say so."

"I do. Now be a good boy and give me some of the limoncello I asked you to bring."

———

Paolo drank limoncello and played cards with Toni until the creeping need to be with Luis overwhelmed him. He bid Toni goodnight and caught the bus. It rumbled through the city at its usual speed, but to Paolo, it crawled. He couldn't bear it. Two stops before home, he jumped off and ran the rest of the way to Luis's bedsit.

It was dark and quiet, but that on its own didn't mean Luis wasn't there. He buzzed the intercom. There was no answer, but as he turned to leave, a kid in a hoodie came out and walked away without checking the exterior door had shut behind him.

Paolo caught it and slipped into the carved-up old terrace that housed Luis's bedsit.

Luis's front door was down the dim corridor. With Luis waiting at the end, it had never seemed too bad, but without him, it was downright creepy. Nerves buzzing, Paolo hurried to Luis's door and knocked. No sound came from inside, but he waited anyway. Counted a hundred heartbeats before he gave up.

He fished his phone from his pocket and called Luis's phone.

It didn't connect.

Despite the plausible possibility that Luis was at the shop or waiting outside Paolo's flat, Paolo's irrational heart sank into the pit of his stomach. Somehow, he'd convinced himself Luis was safe at home, even though Luis's bedsit held nothing but a bed, a single saucepan, and a washing machine jammed into the bathroom. No couch, no TV, and a heating system that couldn't keep Barbados warm. *Please be at my place. I won't ask you anything, I promise.*

But when he got home, Luis wasn't there either.

Paolo trudged upstairs and forced himself to eat. Then he took a beer into the shower and sat down under the hot spray, letting it pummel his neck. *I'm so fucking tired.* But at the same time, restless energy danced under his skin. Anticipation that made no sense, since it was clear Luis wasn't coming. Paolo closed his eyes, willing the hot water to do its job, but it ran out long before it had a hope of soothing the anxiety smouldering in his belly.

He got out of the shower and caught sight of his reflection in the steamed-up mirror. Ever the masochist, he wiped it clean and studied the dark circles beneath eyes that were red and wide with worry. *Stop obsessing over him. He's a grown man. And when he does come back, he'll flip his shit if he thinks you stayed up all night angsting about him.*

When, not if. He could count on that, right?

Paolo had no idea. He shook himself and left the bathroom without bothering to dry off. Damp footprints followed him out, but at his bedroom door, a soft tap from the other end of the hallway turned him around.

He padded to the front door and squinted through the peephole. Luis was already walking away.

Alarmed, Paolo threw the door open. "Where are you going?"

Luis didn't turn around.

Naked but for his towel, Paolo shot after him and grabbed his arm. "Luis. Stop."

Luis whirled around, wrenching his arm free before it seemed to click that it was Paolo.

His expression was like nothing Paolo had ever seen.

Haunted, lost, confused. As if he'd started walking in one direction and ended somewhere entirely different.

Paolo tugged on his arm. "Come in. It's cold."

"You're the one flashing the neighbours."

"Only because you knocked once and walked away three seconds later."

"I knocked three times."

"Why didn't you call then?"

"Thought you'd gone to bed."

Without you? I've forgotten how. Paolo hustled Luis inside and shut the door. Luis reached over his head and slipped the chain on, then bolted it top and bottom.

Paolo eyed Luis as he leant on the door and blew out a long breath. "Expecting burglars?"

"You don't lock your doors at night?"

"You know I don't. Those bolts haven't moved in years."

Luis treated him to a dead-eyed stare, the kind that made it clear he didn't want to explain himself, and Paolo didn't feel like making him. After fretting away his evening, he was just glad Luis had showed up. "Do you want to—"

A gentle finger to his lips quieted him. Luis's other hand moved to Paolo's towel and loosened it enough to unwind it from Paolo's waist. He brought it to Paolo's chest and wiped away the water that still clung to his skin. "You never dry yourself."

Though he was far from cold, Paolo shivered. "I forget."

"Why?"

"It's not important."

"It's cold, P. Of course it's important."

P. Luis had taken to calling Paolo that when his guard

was down. When it was just them, bare skin and nothing else, or at work before the doors opened, and after, when they cleaned up side by side. It was intimate and yet so innocent, Paolo wanted to cry. He let Luis dry every inch of his damp skin and fought the urge to interrupt him with his own wandering hands. He'd learned this about Luis, that sometimes, when he wasn't quite himself, focussing on Paolo seemed to help.

Besides, Paolo was powerless beneath his light touch. He shuddered and closed his eyes, slumping against the wall as his cock hardened and rose, chasing Luis's electric palms. For long minutes, Luis evaded, exploring every inch of Paolo except where he needed him most. Then he closed his hand around Paolo's dick and quickly found a rhythm that had Paolo lurching forward and bracing himself on the opposite wall of the narrow hallway.

Luis slipped into the small space behind him, still working Paolo's cock. "Do you remember when you did this to me? When you turned me inside out with your hands and put your tongue in me?"

Paolo gasped, lost in the pleasure of Luis's wicked touch and, at the same time, blindsided by the filthy turn their encounter had taken. He'd expected Luis to be quiet, silent even, not to kill him with dirty words and sinful hands. "I remember."

"Good." Luis nudged Paolo's legs apart and sank to his knees. He kept his hand on Paolo's cock and softly, like a dream, slipped his tongue inside Paolo.

"*Fuck.*" Paolo's head dropped another inch, and his mouth fell open. Rimming Luis had turned his world upside down, but he'd never considered, despite Luis's fondness for giving out skull-numbing blowjobs, that he might return the favour. Perhaps if he had, he'd have figured somewhere better than the dark hallway as a venue.

Not that it mattered. With his eyes screwed shut, Paolo couldn't see a thing, not even Luis, with his face buried between Paolo's legs. *I need a mirror for this shit.*

Luis drove Paolo wild with his tongue, teasing and light, it set his nerves on fire, only for the steady stroke of his hand on his dick to obliterate them. Paolo's knees turned to jelly. He moaned loud enough for his neighbours to call the police and choked out a warning. "I'm gonna come, fuck, I'm gonna come so hard."

The words had barely left his mouth when his limbs began to seize. White spots danced behind his eyelids, and he came with a harsh groan.

Luis eased off slowly, his hand first, then his tongue. He got to his feet and peeled Paolo from the wall. "Wanna go to bed?"

Paolo stared at him, lost for words despite having so many to say. He nodded and tried to put some semblance of himself back together, but he had nothing, and Luis had everything, even if he didn't want it.

Luis led Paolo to his bedroom and sat him on the edge of his bed. He disappeared to the bathroom while Paolo lay down and gazed at the ceiling, wondering which way was up. He'd grown used to the crazy-hot chemistry he and Luis shared, but what had just happened was off the scale. *And he never even took his clothes off.*

The room was dark. Luis came back and ditched his T-shirt. He was wearing the soft sweatpants he lived in when he wasn't wearing jeans. Paolo waited for him to take them off, but he didn't. He rounded the bed and slipped under the covers.

Bemused, Paolo rolled to face him. Luis had already closed his eyes. *Is that it? He's just gonna show up and rim me into oblivion without a real conversation?* Paolo had lived through worse dates, but nothing about Luis had ever been so trivial. He rolled over, showing his back to Luis in the hope that he'd follow and wrap his arms around him like he always did, as if Paolo was the only thing anchoring him to the earth.

Silence stretched out between them, and for long heartbeats, Luis didn't move. Paolo began to drowse, pulled under by the brain zapping orgasm Luis had gifted him. *I miss him already.* If he'd ever been there at all.

16

"What even is that?" Paolo peered at the spray-painted symbol that had appeared on the pavement outside the cafe. "Is it a compass or a clock? Why has it got no hands? Do you think they forgot? Fucking kids."

Luis pretended not to hear and busied himself with the ketchup bottles, hoping Paolo was thinking out loud rather than starting an actual conversation. He'd been good about that in recent days, leaving Luis alone with his thoughts while Luis distracted him with his hands and mouth, but Luis could tell the oppressive silence was getting to him. That as much as he was trying to understand something he knew nothing about, it wouldn't be long before he snapped, and there wasn't a rim job on earth that would deflect him then.

Paolo shut the cafe door. It was early, not even opening time yet, so he bolted it and came up behind Luis. For once, he didn't slide his hand over Luis's back to warn him he was coming. He didn't do anything. Just stood there for a long moment before he walked away, not realising that Luis could see him in the reflection of the window.

Luis closed his eyes, mourning the lost touch, all the while steeling himself against the wave of relief that flooded him that Paolo hadn't made the connection between Luis and the pocket watch tattooed on the concrete outside, the faceless clock letting Luis know, as if he could forget, that his days and nights with Paolo were numbered. *So just leave already.* It was a no brainer. If Luis wasn't surgically attached to Paolo, it would be easier to keep him out of the mess Dante was trying to make.

At least that's what Luis told himself every afternoon when he left work before Paolo and went home. But by nightfall, the pull to be with Paolo was too strong. Three nights in a row found him on Paolo's doorstep, too strung out to do anything but let Paolo lead him to bed where they slept, wrapped up in each other until it was time to do it all over again. That was the easy part, but then, everything about being naked with Paolo was easy.

The cafe opened for business. By lunchtime, the council had showed up and painted over the pocket watch with crude red paint, leaving a mess far worse than the simple etching.

Paolo returned to the cafe door and scowled at the workers retreating from the sudden rainstorm. "Since when do the council come out and cover graffiti so quick?"

"Gang signs," a customer from the nearest table replied. "They painted over it at the train station too. Funny how they can find the money for that, but not to treat the drug addicts these gangs create."

Paolo shot the woman a sharp glance. "How do you know it's a gang sign?"

The woman shrugged. "They were all over Moss Farm until last week. My son said it's a prison thing, something to do with lost years. I asked him how he knew those things and sent him to school with a bible in his bag, let me tell you."

She said other words and Paolo replied, but Luis really didn't hear them this time, not because he turned his back on them and couldn't follow their lips, but because of his thundering heartbeat. His hands had been shaky since he'd come round from that beatdown with the iron bar. The doctors said it was anxiety, not brain damage, and as Luis flailed over the grill, he finally accepted they might've been right.

He dropped the tongs in the oil-filled frying pan. Cursed, and retrieved them, burning his fingers, *again*. At first he'd been numb to the pain, but not anymore. Everything hurt now, old wounds and new. The scar on his head throbbed, his damaged ear buzzed, and despair lanced his heart so hard his knees went weak.

The cafe door opened and closed. Luis mechanically cooked the orders in front of him. Paolo collected the plates. Luis hyper-focused on scraping the grill and didn't look up until he realised no new order slips had appeared. He didn't need to turn around to know the cafe was empty.

He glanced at the clock. It was a little after two. *What the fuck?* But he sensed Paolo's presence behind him before his brain thought of an answer.

Again, Paolo didn't touch him. Luis spun to face him to

find he wasn't close enough to reach. He was sat at the table by the door, his lovely face twisted into the same suspicion he'd thrown at Luis the first time he'd opened the cafe door. "You want to tell me what's going on?"

"What?"

Paolo slammed his hand down on the table. "Don't fucking do that."

"Do what?"

Paolo stood with a screech of his chair on the tiled floor, and he was in Luis's face before Luis could blink. "Don't come at me with this bullshit that you don't know what I'm talking about. You've been acting weird since your brother showed up, now there's gang graffiti everywhere and you expect me to believe there's nothing going on?"

"There isn't graffiti everywhere. There's one thing outside, and you said it yourself it was probably kids."

"That was before I knew what it was and realised we saw three of them on our way here this morning."

"It was dark this morning."

"Street lamps exist, mate. And this is a city, not a remote village in the mountains."

That morning, like every morning, Luis had been too engrossed in how it felt to hold Paolo's hand to concentrate on his surroundings. They could've walked to the moon and back and he wouldn't have noticed. "I didn't see anything."

"Even if that's true, you saw the one outside, and you know what it means. I know you do; I saw it in your face when that woman told me."

"Oh yeah? What else did you see in my face? Cos you seem to think it's the fucking oracle."

"Don't get tricky with me. I know you're freaking out about something. What did Dante want when he came in?"

"He didn't want anything. If you're so observant, you'd have seen that he didn't eat anything."

"Exactly. He came to see you. Why?"

"Why do you think?"

"I don't know. That's why I'm asking." Paolo's voice rose to a shout by the end of his sentence, and his anger made him impossibly hotter. His cheeks were flushed, and his dark eyes blazed. In any other circumstance, Luis would've jumped him, rolled him to the floor, and fucked him right there, but his scrutiny scared Luis more than Dante did.

"He didn't want anything specific. Just likes winding me up, I've told you that before."

"Have you?"

"Yeah. Maybe you're the one who needs your fucking hearing checked."

Luis pushed past Paolo and stormed into the kitchen, trying to remember if he *had* told Paolo that particular snippet of joy about Dante. They talked a lot, sometimes without Luis realising it was happening, and he'd shared so much with Paolo that it had become a blur. *You should've kept your mouth shut.* For all the good it would've done him. Paolo hadn't needed Luis's confession to know Dante was bad news.

On cue, Paolo barrelled through the kitchen door. "I don't need my hearing checked to know you're losing your mind about something. Do you think I'm asleep when you spend all night staring at the ceiling? That I haven't noticed you're lost in your own head every night you come home and don't talk to me for hours on end? What have I ever done to make you think my head is up my arse so far that I don't give a fuck what's going on with you?"

Paolo had never done anything to make Luis think he didn't care, and that was the problem. He cared so much Luis couldn't hide from him, and that was why this shit had to end. Why he had to get as far away from Paolo as possible before he kicked down Luis's walls and dragged everything out of him.

Tell him you love him.

Luis shook his head to clear it. Where had that come from? He needed to tell Paolo they couldn't see each other anymore. That Luis couldn't work at the cafe and sleep in Paolo's bed. Not that he was so in love with him that he couldn't see himself surviving what he had to do next. "I—"

Paolo cut him off with a growl and shoved him hard enough to make him sway on his feet. "Don't. Whatever deflective rubbish you're about to come out with, just don't. Tell me the truth or don't fucking bother. This is my life too. My business your brother is fucking with to get to you. Why can't you just *talk* to me? Tell me what's going on in your head?"

Something inside Luis snapped. He moved so fast he had Paolo pinned against the wall before he knew what he was doing. "Why do you want to know what's going on in my head? Do you think it belongs to you because I suck your dick? Is that where this is going? You think you can fucking control me?"

Paolo's gaze was wildfire and something else that Luis was too far gone to contemplate. "I don't want to control you. I want to help you."

"Why? So you can mould me to fit your world instead of mine? Do you think it's that easy?"

"None of this is easy, Luis. I just want to understand."

"You don't want to understand. You want to *know* everything. That isn't the same."

"Isn't it? Not everyone has an agenda." Paolo fought Luis's hold on him. He was strong, but Luis was stronger, and he kicked out in frustration, catching Luis's shin with his boot.

The pain opened the gate. Every ounce of fear and despair burst through, and Luis clenched his fists. He pulled his arm back and punched the wall behind Paolo's head. His fist broke through the plasterboard, leaving a hole by Paolo's ear. His knuckles erupted, blood seeping to the surface of his broken skin. Beige dust from the wall littered Paolo's hair. It should've been enough to bring him back to his senses, but it wasn't. Rage still flowed through his veins like lava, and he couldn't think straight.

Luis leaned closer to Paolo, close enough that they could've kissed. "Everyone has an agenda, cos every fucker's out for themself. Sooner you learn that, the sooner you can be done with my shit."

He backed off, every physical disconnect a bullet to his heart. His feet hit the back door.

Paolo stepped forward. "Luis—"

But Luis was already gone. He ripped the door open and fled, pounding the busy streets in the pouring rain until he found himself on the dilapidated street he called home. Wet through and breathless, he stopped and doubled over, shock and cold slamming into him like a sucker punch. *What have I done?* Paolo hadn't flinched at Luis's flying fists, but the damage to the wall was the same as if Luis had punched him in the face. The cafe was everything to him, to his family, and Luis had brought trouble to their door. He *was* the fucking trouble. Paolo had been right about him from the start.

Nausea rolled through Luis. He forced himself upright and trudged to the bedsit. The front door of the old house was half hidden by the overgrown trees by the porch. It took him a moment to notice the blood-red spray paint covering the battered wood—another faceless clock, this time with a crude interpretation of the Italian flag blotted into it. A marker or a warning, it didn't matter. Dante's message was clear: *fuck this up and I'll kill him.*

———

Luis didn't come back. It was becoming such a theme, Paolo was almost bored, but this time felt different. He locked the cafe without wondering if he should wait in case Luis returned, and went home. Shut the door behind him. Bolted it. Only then did the magnitude of what had happened hit him full force.

Trembling, he sank to the floor to sit with his head in his hands, his back to the door. *What the hell just happened?*

He pictured Luis's face as he'd driven his fist into the wall, the desperation, the fear, all twisted up to make a man Paolo didn't recognise.

A sob coughed out of his chest, dry and pointless. *The fuck are you crying for? You pushed him into it. You laid hands on him first.* As if that made it better. Luis had wanted Paolo to be scared of him, as if manhandling him and punching the wall would prove he really was the man Paolo had naïvely feared him to be.

But it didn't work. Paolo *was* scared, not of Luis, but *for* Luis. Something had happened to push him like that, and as guilty as Paolo felt for tipping him over the edge, he knew it wasn't him. He was a catalyst, not the source. Nah, that was Dante. It had always been Dante.

Paolo lifted his head from his hands and banged it against the door. White powder from the plaster Luis had pulverised drifted down from his hair and landed on his knees. He drew a clock face into it, then scrubbed it out. Anxiety like he'd never felt flared hotly in his chest. He was bone tired, but at the same time buzzing with enough nervous energy to power a space station.

The temptation to chase Luis down was so strong he almost choked on it. He clenched his eyes shut and banged his head again. *God, I wish I didn't love him.*

But Paolo did love him, more than he could ever say. *I need to help him.* But how? Short of murdering Dante, there was nothing Paolo could do.

A humourless snort broke the silence in the empty flat. Paolo imagined himself storming Dante's Moss Farm tower block and throttling him as he slept. It was a comforting image, but only for a moment. Hurting Dante —as if eating bacon every day had given Paolo the superpowers he'd need to take on a drug lord—would make him no better than the world Luis needed so desperately to escape. It would make him one of them, forever, and there'd be no coming back. No safe place for Luis to lay his head when it was all over. No warm arms to let him know how much he was loved. That he mattered. And that nothing he'd done, or could ever do, would change that.

He needs to know I love him, now more than ever. But as hard as he tried, Paolo couldn't see a way he'd ever get to tell him.

17

The flat smelt the same as it always had: of boiled eggs and weed smoke. Luis hadn't noticed the last time he'd been there, but as he traced the road map with a pencil, marking out escape routes if Dante's exchange went south, it choked him.

"Why are you even doing that?" Dante called from the sofa. "You know we've got Google Maps and shit these days, right?"

Luis ignored him. He didn't know how visible Dante was on the police radar, but he didn't fancy carrying an electronic log of every search he'd made in his pocket. He could burn physical maps before he set off. Buy his train ticket with cash and his hood obscuring his face. It wasn't a fool-proof plan, but it was better than nothing. And more than Dante had offered him. "Why Coventry?" he asked suddenly. "I thought the Albanians got their link from the Leicester boys."

Dante kept his gaze on the TV. "They do. But only cos no one's offered them a better price."

"That's because no one's stupid enough to take on a crew that big."

Dante grunted.

Luis eyed him from the kitchen table. "Please tell me *you're* not that stupid?"

"What do you care?"

"I don't care about you. But you're not the one carrying, are you? You haven't got the balls to run that shit yourself. You never have."

"Don't need to, do I?"

"If you did, you'd be working at McDonalds by now."

Dante hauled himself from his couch and sauntered to the table where Luis sat. He peered at the maps with stone cold disinterest. "What's the matter? Missing your boy toy? Fucking sap. You've only been apart a few hours."

If only. It had been six days since Luis had walked out on Paolo, and he missed him so much he felt physically sick every moment he was awake. Sleeping forever seemed the ideal solution, but his brain wouldn't play ball with that either. For days and days, he'd paced the bedsit and roamed the streets at night, but still he couldn't sleep. Some nights, he passed the cafe and watched Paolo lock up and leave. It took strength he didn't know he had to stop himself following him home. Only the fear that he'd be seen stopped him. Evidence to discredit the lie he was about to tell. "He's not my boy toy anymore. I stopped banging him a week ago."

Dante's grin turned lizard-like. "That so?"

"Yeah. And don't pretend you don't already know. I know you've got eyes on me."

"What about your cushty job?"

"What job? I quit like you told me to. Besides, don't need a job, do I? I got you."

Despite Luis's best efforts, sarcasm weighted every damn syllable, but Dante didn't flinch. "That's right. You've got me, and I've got you. That's what families are for, right?"

"If you say so."

Luis went back to scanning the map. He was only there because Dante had insisted he needed to be to learn the details of the clusterfuck the next phase of his life was bound to be, but so far, he'd toyed with Luis for hours and told him nothing except the city where the kilo of coke would be exchanged. No when or why. Another day wasted.

A day Luis could've spent with Paolo.

The map blurred as he let his mind drift to the last time they'd been together and Luis had been present enough to enjoy it. Swathes of smooth olive skin stretched out before him, sheened with sweat as Luis explored Paolo with his tongue, absorbing every shudder and moan, committing them to memory. Deep down, he'd always known the day would come when those memories were all he had left, but fuck, he wasn't ready. He'd never be fucking ready.

Eventually, Dante deigned to tell him the muling op was set up for two days' time. "You've got forty-eight hours to get your shit together. Then I need you at the pick-up by four."

"In the morning?"

"Yeah. You can blend in with the commuters that way, right?"

"As opposed to the drunks at night?"

"If you were a copper, which train would you search?"

"If I was a copper, I'd have dropped you in the sea."

"Liar. You love me really."

"I don't." Luis folded the map and tucked it into his pocket. "I wish you were dead."

It felt good to say, even if they were wasted words Dante would never take seriously. Hate simmered hotly in Luis's veins. *I could do it right now. Kick his fucking head in so he'd never wake up.* But aside from the reasons he hadn't already killed Dante, Luis knew how it felt to hurt a man that way, and he couldn't live with more guilt.

He made for the door.

Somehow, Dante got there first and blocked his way. "I figured you'd pretend to ditch your man and your job, but you look heartsick, man. Don't tell me you actually cut him loose for real?"

"What makes you think *he* didn't cut me loose after you started fucking with his business?"

"Cos no one turns away Pope dick, man. You know that."

Luis cringed. "Whatever. It isn't a thing anymore, so you can stop giving a shit. You got what you wanted. I'm unemployed and at your disposal."

"Yeah, but you're no good to me if you're obsessing over a lost piece of ass. I know how that goes."

"How? You don't care about anyone but yourself."

"No, but I had to deal with Asa's soft self when you stopped fucking him, so . . ."

"What?"

Dante laughed. "You think I didn't know about that? Man, you live in a fucking bubble, don't you? Who do you think told him to come on to you in the first place?"

Luis's head was too full of Paolo to process much else, let alone the nonsense that spewed from Dante's mouth, but still he tried. "That makes no sense. I got drunk and fucked Asa once—"

"It was more than that."

"Whatever. It was ten years ago. The fuck has that got to do with you?"

Dante shrugged. "I'd seen you eyeing him up, so I told him to get you drunk and into your bed. With you disappearing every couple of days to scratch your itch, it seemed like the ideal solution."

"Yeah? How did that pan out for you?"

"It didn't cos he couldn't keep your interest. But that's not my point."

"What is your point?" Luis asked wearily. "Because if all you're trying to do is demonstrate that you've manipulated me my whole god damn life, you can stop now. I already know."

"And yet you're still here." Dante leaned back on the door he was blocking. "Why is that?"

Because despite that fact that you're weak as fuck, I'm still terrified you'll hurt the man I love. "I need money. How much you giving me for this transport shit?"

"Nothing. You'll get your cut when it's sold."

"I can't wait that long." Luis could wait a hundred years for dirty drug money, but if he couldn't convince Dante it was all he cared about, the game was up. "I got sacked, remember? No back pay, and I need to make rent now he's not paying it for me."

"You can live here."

"No."

"Why not? I need you close if you're going to be my wingman again."

"I was never your wingman. I was just an idiot who did as he was told."

"And now?"

"Now I'm an idiot who needs to pay rent, so give me some fucking money."

Dante kept his gaze locked with Luis's as he slid his hand into his pocket. He came up with a thick roll of notes that made Luis's heart leap and sink at the same time. A fraction of that sum would've set him for a year, but the knowledge of where it had come from made him want to die. He didn't want Dante's money any more than he wanted his love.

"How much do you need?" Dante asked.

Unable to speak, Luis shrugged. Dante peeled off an amount that was more than Luis would need for the next three months. He held it out. "This do you?"

Luis took the money and shoved it in his pocket. "It'll do. Now move."

Dante stayed put. "I'm not moving till you give me some honesty about that dude you've been tapping. Is he something I still got to worry about?"

"I already told you it's done. Why are you so obsessed with him? You wanna bang him too?"

"Would you care if I did?"

Rage blazed through Luis, sharp and true, and he fought to swallow it down. Dante was as straight as he'd once thought Asa to be, but he'd fuck anyone to get what he wanted. Shame he didn't seem to know Paolo would set himself on fire before he let Dante into his bed. Luis too, for that matter, considering their last encounter had seen Luis's fist break a wall that didn't belong to him.

Shame replaced the fury bubbling in his chest. He hadn't frightened Paolo—fuck no—but he'd hurt him and tainted every moment they'd ever spent together by regressing to the stupid boy who'd followed Dante all the way to a fucking prison cell. And now here they were, about to go back in time and do it all over again.

Genius. If it hadn't been so tragic, Luis might've laughed. But there was nothing funny about the leer twisting Dante's face. It shot arrows through Luis's armour, shattering his tenuous grip on his self-control. Anger rose again. He gripped Dante's shirt and hurled him away from the door, far harder than he'd shoved Paolo more than a week ago, but nowhere near hard enough.

Dante stumbled, shoulder colliding with the wall. He slid to the floor, amusement and pain fighting for dominance on his smug face. "So you would care? Funny that, when you're saying he's sacked you off and kicked you out of his bed. Maybe I can't trust you after all."

"I never said you could trust me," Luis ground out. "Get Asa to put a bullet in my head for all I care. I don't give a fuck anymore."

Leaving Dante on the floor, he wrenched the door open. Asa stood on the other side, face a study in apathy, but Luis remembered taking him apart well enough to see the signs that he'd heard every word. The creases beneath his ocean-blue eyes, the tick in his strong jaw. Luis had liked him once, cared about him even. But now he knew he was no better than Dante; the sight of him fed the beast Dante had awakened.

Luis barrelled into him, crowding him against the balcony railing. "What do you want, Asa? You want to bend over for me, or my brother?"

Asa easily had two stone on Luis, but he didn't fight Luis's hold on him. His gaze darted to the end of the corridor. "You need to get out of here, man. If Martell comes back, he'll cut you up, no questions asked."

"I'm not that lucky. My brother doesn't want me dead. It would spoil his fun . . . you know, the kind of fun that has him send cash-hungry motherfuckers to my bed?"

Asa swallowed thickly. "It wasn't just about that. But you know how he is, I didn't have a choice."

There was nothing Luis didn't understand about that. It was his entire life wrapped up in one sentence. But Dante had bled him dry. He had nothing left for Asa. He slammed him against the railings again. "I don't give a fuck why you suck my brother's dick, metaphorical or otherwise, just stay the hell out of my way."

He let Asa go and strode down the corridor until he came to the stairs. Martell stepped onto the landing. He shot Luis major side-eye. Luis ignored him and jogged down the stairs and out of the building. Let Martell chase him down and stick a knife between his ribs. Luis wouldn't hear him coming, and he didn't care. Heaviness dragged in his gut. His legs slowed.

Fuck, I really don't.

With shaking hands, he pulled the cash Dante had given from his pocket and dumped it in a nearby bin, but even without it burning a hole in his pocket, it still followed him as he walked away. The fresh air of the outside world became a suffocating cloud of invisible smoke. Acrid and thick, it filled his throat, closing it off like he was breathing through a straw of an orange Capri-Sun, the only thing him and Dante had ever drunk until they'd figured out how to break into Ma's gin cabinet.

Luis's lungs heaved. He was a mile away from the bedsit, and his legs weren't working.

The cafe was around the next corner. The temptation to stumble back into Paolo's life was so strong Luis could taste it, but the memory of Dante's leer won out. Staying away from Paolo was the only way. Perhaps one day, after—

No. Don't you get it? You never fit with his life in the first place. He deserves better than you. Luis thought of Nonna pottering around her room at the nursing home with no clue half the time who Paolo was. Of Toni scowling at any soul who dared to come near him, saving his good humour for Paolo and Luis. *Fuck, they all do.*

Somehow, Luis made it home. The exterior door had been busted down a few nights before—a police raid on the ganja dude upstairs—and was still wide open. Luis ducked into the house and hurried to his own front door. The bedsit was the same spartan piece of shit it had been since he'd moved in, but without Paolo keeping him warm, the barren walls had become his only sanctuary.

He shut the door behind him and leant against it, closing his eyes. The battered wood was warm to his numb skin. Paolo's storage-heater sorcery had worked, and the bedsit was no longer as cold as it was outside.

Neither was Luis's heart. Or his nerves as they jangled and buzzed, alive with a fear that had nothing to do with the imminent drugs run.

He pushed off the door and drifted to the kitchen. His legs still felt weak, and his hands still shook. *You need to eat.* He opened the cupboard and stared, unseeing, at the handful of provisions leftover from the last time he'd shopped. *When was that?* Damn, he had no idea. And he wasn't hungry. Hadn't been since the last meal he'd shared with Paolo.

But he had to eat. Tomorrow he'd need his wits about him, not to be on his knees with low blood sugar.

He opened a can of spaghetti hoops and emptied it into his only saucepan. The hob was slow to heat. Lights off, Luis gripped the counter and let his eyes fall closed again, wondering if it was possible to fall asleep standing up. If, perhaps, after days of tossing and turning in his lumpy bed, this was the answer, a slow, hypnotic sway over a tin of Heinz.

The metallic snap of the letterbox roused him. Startled, he opened his eyes to find the carby orange gloop in the saucepan was boiling. He turned it off and ventured into the hallway. An envelope was on the floor by the front door.

He picked it up and turned it over. His name was scrawled on one side, and it was sealed shut with thick brown parcel tape. *Jesus fucking Christ, please tell me that bellend hasn't dropped the package off here . . .*

But the thought tailed off as Luis looked closer at his scribbled name. At the exaggerated capital letters and barely legible lowercase. He knew that handwriting. He'd spent the last two months staring at it, deciphering it, and producing plates of food in the hope that he'd got it right. *"Should've been a doctor, right? Shame I'm all beauty and no brains."*

Paolo's face, alive with his sardonic grin, flashed into Luis's brain, filling every sense and facet. Heart pounding, he tore the envelope open. Bank notes, twenties and tens, fluttered to the floor, along with Luis's rent card and a scrap of paper torn from the cafe's order pad. Luis ignored the card and the money and scrambled for the note.

Luis,

Here's your wages from the last however long. I don't even know, but your tax records are up to date, so there's that. I hope you're okay and enjoying whatever you're doing now. Let me know if you need a reference and I'll post it to you.

P

The note slipped from Luis's fingers. He slid slowly to the floor, surrounded by money he'd earned with honest graft, early mornings and long days spent side by side with a man who'd claimed a long-dead piece of his heart. A new ache tore a hole in Luis's chest.

With a guttural moan, he put his head in his hands and cried.

18

Paolo strode away from Luis's bedsit, rain driving into his face, disguising the angry tears enough that he could pretend they weren't there. On the way over, he'd pictured reaching for the letterbox and the door opening at just the right moment. Luis meeting his gaze, and everything that had torn them apart disappearing as if it had never been there at all.

His imagination hadn't counted on Luis not being home, but as he left the dark bedsit behind without bothering to knock, the cynic in him reasoned that it was just as well. Their last encounter had turned violent, and Luis had walked away. Worse, Paolo had let him and had done nothing to fix it in six long days. How did they come back from that?

We don't. He doesn't want your life, and you don't want his. It sounded so simple on those terms, but the words scraped Paolo's soul. It was true; he didn't want to be part of the world Luis had come from, but he didn't believe Luis did either. He *couldn't* believe that the growing, innocent pride he'd seen in Luis every day he'd worked at the cafe hadn't been real. It wasn't Paolo's place to proclaim a bacon sandwich worth more than whatever bullshit Dante Pope was peddling, but fuck, to Luis it was. It had to be, or Paolo really had shared his bed with a stranger.

Lost, Paolo caught the bus home. With all the stops, it was a five-minute journey, but the rush hour traffic was backed up to the cash-and-carry. Paolo found a window seat and settled in, tipping his head against the steamed-up glass and watching his tiny slice of the city go by without seeing a single thing. Luis was like a vice around his heart, clenching tighter and tighter the further Paolo got from the bedsit. *What is it about this dude?* Paolo could admit to himself that he loved Luis, but he'd loved others before. Wanted them. Needed them. But he'd never loved anyone like he loved Luis. Never with so much of himself and so little left behind now Luis was gone.

He's not gone, though, is he? It's not like he's died.

Felt like it, though.

Paolo's gaze fell on the cafe as the high street came into view. The council paint on the pavement was still there, clumsily plastered over the message Dante's crew had left on the concrete. He still had no clue what it meant. Just that it had frightened Luis enough to push him over the edge and drive him away from Paolo for good. Had that been Dante's intention? Or had it been a warning to Luis about something else? Something deeper and more sinister than Paolo could imagine. He wasn't sure he wanted to know, but he couldn't seem to let it go. Couldn't let *Luis* go. This couldn't be it. There had to be something else he could do.

But what? He'd paid Luis up to date. Filed his taxes. Tapped out a dozen messages he'd never sent. Spent hours at a time with his thumb hovering over Luis's number. *Call him. Worse-case scenario, he doesn't answer. And* Paolo could've handled a tangible reason to give up and walk away. This silence? Nah. It was killing him.

The bus rolled into the high street. Paolo shuffled off and started in the direction of home. He'd already been to see Nonna, and all he had left to do was eat a solitary dinner and fall into his empty bed, but his feet dragged as he neared the flat, and the sense of something undone nagged at him so profoundly his head ached. Dante replaced Luis in his mind. Anger came again, white hot and pointless. Paolo wanted to hurt him more than he'd ever wanted to hurt anyone. Wanted to stamp on his smug face. Set fire to whatever it was that mattered more than his own brother.

But beneath Paolo's rage, common sense was a cool drip of cleansing water. There was nothing he could do to hurt Dante, but perhaps he could reach him another way. Perhaps—

Don't be a fool. But Paolo had been a fool for Luis the split second he'd found him waiting at the counter looking for work. For a job Toni had persuaded Paolo to give him. Maybe if Paolo'd had faith in Luis from the start, Dante would never have got to him. Who the hell knew? With so many questions unanswered, wild speculation was all Paolo had.

Didn't stop you filing his P45, did it?

Guilt prickled Paolo's skin. He'd done that on the fifth day Luis hadn't shown up for work, angrily hacking away at his laptop, four beers deep. He'd regretted it come the morning, but the damage was done. It was official. Luis no longer worked for him.

Paolo wondered if Luis would even care when the tax forms came through. If the security of employment had ever meant anything to him. Then he remembered every tiny thing about Luis that kept him up at night, and his feet finally took root in the pavement and turned him around.

Fuck this. I'm gonna tell that cunt straight.

———

The Moss Farm estate towered over Paolo's corner of the city. Literally. Six blocks of grimy bricks and dodgy cladding cast shadows over the streets below, grim and imposing, but a lifeline to anyone who couldn't afford to live anywhere else.

Dante Pope could definitely afford to live elsewhere, but Paolo had it on good authority that he still resided in the council flat Luis had grown up in. Block three, top floor. He imagined it would be obvious which number.

He reached the bottom of the towers, a haunting maze of boarded-up windows and gang graffiti. Toni's favourite betting shop beside the launderette was long gone, but

Paolo could still smell the sausage rolls they'd served there to keep punters betting past lunchtime. Greasy and soaked in ketchup, they'd been the best non-Italian thing he'd eaten until he'd discovered the joys of an English bacon sandwich.

Block three was tucked away behind the run-down play park. The usual clutch of teens hung around outside, but the vibe was different to the aimless congregation outside the other blocks. These youths had purpose. They came and went with an efficiency that was hard to believe. *They're working. For Dante.* Of course they were. Why do your own dirty work when you could pay a kid to do it for you?

More nausea rattled Paolo's gut. He swallowed it down —*focus*—and approached the entrance.

Older youths stood near the lifts, smoking and observing. They tracked Paolo to the stairs, and he wasn't surprised when one of them broke off and followed him. He'd watched enough *Top Boy* to know their job was to track every face that came in and out of the block.

He trudged to the top storey, past every stairwell with watching eyes. The uppermost floor was guarded like a vault. Men dressed in black blocked the corridor and stared Paolo down as he approached.

Undeterred, he stopped in front of them. "I'm here to see Dante."

"Who?"

Paolo rolled his eyes. "Dante. I'm Paolo from Toni's cafe on the high street. I know his brother."

"Whose? Dante's or Toni's?"

"Very funny. Just tell him I'm here, will you?"

The biggest man smirked, but the slighter one pulled his phone from his pocket and disappeared down the corridor.

Paolo prepared for a silent wait, but the big man stepped away from his post and caught Paolo's arm.

"Are you really friends with Luis? Cos if you're not, you're gonna get hurt. This ain't the place to play games. Martell won't like it, and he'll kick the shit out of you when he comes back."

Paolo eyed the large hand gripping his elbow. The man it belonged to was pretty hot, at least, Paolo would've thought so before Luis. As it was, all he thought was that the strong hand belonged to the wrong person. He shook it off. "We're really friends. Who are you?"

"Asa."

"Are *you* friends with Luis?"

"I was, once upon a time, which is why I know you coming here is a bad idea. Dante already—"

Footsteps behind Asa cut him off. He moved quickly to reclaim his position, and by the time his sidekick reappeared, it was as if the exchange had never happened. Asa stared straight ahead, and Paolo turned his attention to Martell, relieved to see his expression had lost its harsh edges.

"You checked out," he said. "Leave your shoes by the door."

"Which door?"

Asa's smirk returned. "114. It's the one at the end."

He stepped aside and waved Paolo through. His

humour remained, but Martell's stare was hard enough to make Paolo nervous. Paying Dante an unannounced visit had seemed like a good idea when he'd been all rage and righteousness, but it was a massive risk. The only facts Paolo knew about Dante was that he was a gaping arsehole who'd thrown his little brother to the wolves. He had zero clue how he'd react or what he'd do if he decided Paolo was the last person on earth he wanted to see.

Flat 114 was exactly where Asa had said it would be. The door was open. Paolo slipped inside, toed off his shoes, and followed the sound of voices into the living room. He imagined walking into a room full of muscle men, tooled up, with mean mugs and piles of cash in front of them, but he found Dante Pope alone, stretched out on an obnoxious couch, watching *Bargain Hunt* in his underwear.

Paolo forced himself to look. Dante'd had plenty of time to put his clothes on. He'd left them off for a reason, but if he was trying to make Paolo uncomfortable, he'd fail. Dante had the same strong arms and tattooed skin as Luis, but the similarities ended there. Luis's gaze was often so haunted it was hard to see anything else in him, but when his guard was down, he had kind, honest eyes.

Dante's were sharp and cold and didn't match the big smile he broke out for Paolo. "So, I was right."

Paolo stopped by the coffee table. "Right about what?"

"About you and my brother. Asa told me Luis doesn't do relationships, but I know my brother's got a soft heart, and you're just his type."

"How do you know what his type is? He's been in prison for six years."

"And I knew him for twenty before he went down. Of course, he never had an actual boyfriend, but I saw the dudes that would catch his eye. Always the dark ones. I prefer blondes myself, and tits. Nice big tits."

"Good for you."

Dante snagged a joint from an ashtray on the table and offered it to Paolo.

Paolo waved it away. As tempting as it was to take the edge off the agitation scraping his insides, he needed a clear head. "I want to talk to you about Luis."

"Of course you do. What's the problem? Is he not washing your dishes well enough?"

"Luis is a good worker."

"I know that. He used to work for me."

"Are you trying to get him to work for you again?"

Dante lit up and blew smoke in Paolo's face. "Why would you say that?"

Because he's out there somewhere losing his fucking mind, when he should be safe at home with me. "Because he's . . . distracted. And your visit the other week freaked him out. Why did you come?"

"Not a crime to visit your baby brother at work, is it?"

"No, but if you were that fussed, you'd have showed up months ago."

"If you think that, then you don't know Luis at all. He didn't want to see me when he first got out. Otherwise, you'd have seen my face at the start."

"Why did I see your face at all? Why can't you just leave him alone?"

"Is that what he said to you? That he wants me to leave him alone?"

Sensing a trap, Paolo went with the truth. "He hasn't said anything to me."

"So why are you so sure I'm the problem? My brother's a complicated person, man. Dude is never happy unless he's fucking miserable."

"Maybe you've never given him the chance to be anything else."

"Expert on my brother, are you?"

He had Paolo there. The only masterclass he could give on Luis was how to make him come in two minutes flat, and even that was only when Luis wanted him to. When he didn't get to Paolo first and make him such a juddering mess he didn't know which way was up. "I'm not saying that."

Dante smoked more of his joint, regarding Paolo with lazy, weed-hazed eyes. "Do you know what I think, homie?"

Paolo fought the urge to roll his eyes. "Go on."

"I think you're a convenient hole for my brother to get his dick wet while he figures out how to be a real man again. That prison shit got him good, though you're not the first pretty boy to turn his head on the outside, so don't be thinking you're special."

"What if you're wrong?"

"Then I'm wrong, and you get your way, don't you?"

"You'd leave him alone if he asked you to?"

"That's not what I said."

The weed smoke was getting to Paolo. His brain worked sluggishly to collate anything Dante had said that actually made sense. "What are you saying then?"

Dante sat back on his vulgar couch and spread his legs. "Does it matter? What people say isn't important, it's what they do. But I have an offer for you if you want to negotiate, pretty boy."

Paolo's gaze drifted to Dante's crotch, to his cock, where it strained against his underwear, and hysterical laughter bubbled out of his chest. "Are you for real? You want me to suck *your* dick? Yeah, okay, mate. I'll jump right on that."

Dante moved like a snake. He lunged from the couch, grabbed Paolo by the throat, and shoved him against the TV unit. He lacked Luis's strength, but knowing there was a posse of rude boys outside the flat, Paolo let it happen.

He fell slack in Dante's grasp, resisting the urge to break free and punch him in the face.

Dante leered. "I wasn't asking you to suck my dick, bro. I don't swing that way."

"What were you asking me then?"

"I wasn't asking you nothing. I'm telling you. My brother's a road man, and he makes his own choices. The Luis I know would lose his shit if he knew his little bitch was up in my face making claims on him like this, so why don't you take your homo self out of here before you get hurt?"

Frustration ripped through Paolo. He squirmed in Dante's hold. "You really don't care, do you?"

"About what? Your opinion on what my brother should be doing?"

"It's not my opinion. It's got nothing to do with me."

"So why are you here? Why are you in my yard talking about sucking my dick when my family business doesn't concern you?"

"I don't give a fuck about your business. I only care about Luis, and you've got to know whatever you're doing to him is fucking him up. You can't be so dense that you don't understand that."

Dante snorted. "That kid has always been fucked up. It don't matter if he's on the road or working at the damn supermarket, he's never going to change, so if you're waiting for him to turn into your ideal husband or whatever, you're wasting your time."

Paolo was beginning to believe he really was wasting his time, but not with Luis. It was Dante who was a gold-star oxygen thief, and the urge to tell him so danced with Paolo's simmering temper. Only the knowledge that he'd be playing into Dante's hands kept him quiet. *Talk to him like he's human. You might be the only one who ever bothers.* But there was a reason for that. Dante wasn't human. He was a cold pit of a man who'd forgotten how to be anything else. "Please," Paolo ground out through gritted teeth. "Just leave him alone. He did his time for you so you could get on with whatever bullshit you do out here. Six years of his life. For you. Why can't you just let him go?"

Dante's expression changed. For a fleeting moment, he looked just like Luis; hurt, bewildered, and so lost Paolo almost felt sorry for him. But a heartbeat later, his face morphed back to the icy sneer that made Paolo hate him so much. "Newsflash, *Paolo*. Luis didn't serve that time for me. He took the years to *get away from me*. Told me himself, so guess what? That's how we roll now, so if your boy wants out of the life, he's gonna have to do more years in the box, you feel me? And don't count on him making it out alive this time. I got shanks everywhere, man."

Paolo wasn't up to speed on street talk, but the sentiment wasn't lost on him. And it was clear the conversation was over.

Dante let him go.

Paolo straightened his rumpled clothes and walked to the door. With his hand on the cheap wood, he turned back, but Dante had already lit another smoke and reclaimed his place in front of the TV. He didn't look up as Paolo backed out of the flat and left.

Outside, Asa escorted him down the stairs. Paolo ignored him, desperate to escape the stuffy building and feel the winter wind on his skin, as if it could cleanse him of Dante's spiteful apathy. He felt dirty, inside and out. Scared, too. Dante was a caricature gangster, straight from a cartoon joke book. Alone, he was nothing. But Dante Pope was never alone. He had a network of mash men at his disposal. Men who'd cut someone to bits if Dante told them to. Cut *Luis* to bits. Until that moment, Paolo had never believed Dante would hurt Luis in that way.

What if Paolo had changed his mind?

Brain racing, Paolo drifted home. Only the vague memory that he needed something from the shop stopped him going straight there.

He ducked into the Londis at the end of the high street. The after-work queue for cheap booze was long. Paolo considered joining them, but he'd been drunk all week, and his body was starting to protest. Running a cafe solo didn't mix well with a skinful the night before.

Head down, he retreated to the chilled aisle and picked up a bottle of milk. A big one. Like Luis still spent days and days at his flat, brewing Paolo strong instant coffee while he drank his builder's tea. *Idiot. Stop acting like he shared your bed your entire adult life.*

Paolo put the big bottle back and reached for the smallest one. There were other things he needed too, but he lacked the brain power to remember them.

The till was at the front of the shop. He joined the queue and scrolled through his phone to occupy himself while he waited. Nonna had sent him a garbled message from her ancient Nokia. No words, just random symbols and letters. He deleted it and opened the WhatsApp from Toni instead. Regretted it. *Jesus. How many times is he gonna ask for Luis?* Four, so far, and Paolo was running out of fibs to explain his absence. Sooner or later, he'd have to tell Toni the truth, but not yet. An Italian inquisition was something else, and Paolo didn't have the spoons.

Gaze still on his phone, he moved forwards with the queue and straight into the back of the woman in front. "Sorry."

The old woman shook her head. "You young people, obsessed with your phones. It's a wonder more of you don't get hit by the bus."

Paolo opened his mouth to argue, but a tall figure at

the till caught his attention. Dressed in sweats and a familiar grey hoodie, the man had a profile Paolo would've recognised anywhere. *Luis.* Somehow, Paolo had convinced himself he really would never see him again, and he was ridiculously unprepared. His heart flipped, his mouth went dry, and his phone slipped from his fingers, clattering to the floor.

He bent to retrieve it. The old woman beat him to it and passed it over with another shake of her head.

Paolo grabbed the phone and lurched to his feet, but Luis had already left.

Milk forgotten, Paolo ditched it on the nearest shelf and fled the shop. He dashed out into the rain and checked in every direction for which way Luis had gone, but he was nowhere to be seen. Cursing, Paolo took a chance and headed in the opposite direction to Luis's bedsit and towards his own flat, hoping beyond hope that perhaps Luis hadn't gone home.

Despite the rain, the high street was lively with drinkers spilling out of the pubs and bars. Paolo shouldered through them and out through the park by the post office. The wind was fierce. Coupled with the howling rain, it forced his head down, and he was almost right on top of the bench before he spotted the slumped broad shoulders and hunched back.

For the second time in ten minutes, the sight of Luis stopped Paolo's heart. He took a deep breath and let it out slowly. Logic told him to walk on by. That if Luis wanted to see him, he'd have come knocking by now or picked up the phone. But ordinary logic didn't work for Luis. If Paolo wanted to fix this, he had to do it himself.

He took the long way round the bench so Luis would see him coming, but with his head down and his eyes half closed, Luis didn't seem to notice.

Paolo stopped in front of him and crouched down, resisting the urge to put his hands on Luis's knees, but barely. "Hey."

Luis blinked. "Hey."

"Why are you sitting in the rain?"

"Why not? Cheaper than a shower."

"Aren't you cold?"

Luis shrugged. Of course he did, and fondness warred with frustration in the gigantic Luis-section of Paolo's heart.

Paolo shook his head. "You're nuts."

"Am I?"

"Yeah. It's fucking freezing out here."

"Good job I've got your hoodie then, isn't it? Unless you want it back? Is that why you're here?"

"What do you think?"

"I think I should give you the hoodie." Luis emptied the pockets of keys, his phone, and an unopened pack of cigarettes. "You want your phone too? I kind of forgot it was yours in the first place."

"It's not mine. I gave it to you."

"You lent it to me so you could get hold of your employee."

"Don't be like that."

"Like what?"

"Like that's all we've got. You don't want the job, that's fine, but it doesn't mean we can't be friends."

"Friends don't push each other around like I did to you. And they don't bring trouble to your door, so I'm guessing you should call me something else." Luis stood and unzipped Paolo's hoodie. He took it off and held it out. "I'll give you your phone back as soon as I can."

"I don't want the phone, and I don't want this either." Paolo pushed the hoodie away. "Why are you being like this? What's he done to you?"

"Who?"

"Your dickhead brother. I know he's holding something over you."

"You don't know shit."

"Then tell me," Paolo snapped. "If you don't want me, I can't argue with that, but don't walk out on a job you actually like because of him . . . *or* because of me. You don't have to suck my dick to work for me. I told you a hundred times the two things aren't connected."

He was shouting by the time he was done, and some of the handful of people who were in the park swivelled round to look at them.

Luis didn't seem to notice. He stared at Paolo like he'd grown mutant horns. "You think I left because of you?"

"No, I think you left for lots of reasons, and I get that most of them are none of my business, but I got up in your face and backed you into a corner. I know that now, and I'm sorry."

Luis said nothing. His gaze grew distant again with zero clue of what he was thinking, and the will to keep fighting him drained from Paolo so abruptly he almost fell over.

He belatedly realised he was still crouching on the ground and stood, facing Luis at eye level. "Look, I'm the one who escalated what happened at work. So don't be apologising for that when it was my fault."

"It wasn't your fault."

"It—" Paolo swallowed down another wave of frustration. "Whatever. It doesn't matter. All I'm saying is there's a job for you if you still want it. No strings, no obligations. And no more twenty questions, okay? I get that you don't want me in your life like that."

Luis shook his head. "You don't know shit about what I want."

"Then tell me."

"I can't."

"Why not?"

"Because I can't!" Luis's voice rose enough for it to crack, and he flinched, as if he'd never heard himself shout before. "I just fucking can't. I love— *Fuck!* Just leave it, okay? Leave *me*. Whatever you think you want from me, it's not fucking worth it."

Paolo took every syllable of Luis's expletive laden despair like a bullet to the gut, and helplessness replaced his anger. He didn't know what to do. He never had. All he'd done was flail around in his feelings with no clue what they actually meant in real life. He loved Luis, of that he was certain, but what good was that when Luis was drowning in something Paolo could never be part of?

Tears stung his eyes, making him thankful again for the rain.

Luis shivered, and Paolo couldn't bear it. He found Luis's cold hand, squeezed it tight, and uttered words he'd spoken once before on a night that had felt like the beginning of something, not the end. "Come home with me . . . please?"

19

Luis was soaked through, they both were. Paolo boiled the kettle before he remembered he'd left the milk at the shop. *Genius.*

He found two beers at the back of the fridge that were cold enough to give them both pneumonia, and took them to the bedroom. Luis sat on the edge of the bed like an unexploded bomb, tension straining every part of him Paolo could see. Paolo put the beers on the bedside table and nudged his way between Luis's legs. "Relax. We can just go to sleep. You feel safe here, right?"

"Safe?"

"Yeah. That's all I want. For you to know you can be here anytime you want and it's always okay."

"It's not okay, though, is it?"

"It is right now. Anything else can suck a bag till morning."

A faint grin threatened Luis's grim expression. He slid

his hands up the backs of Paolo's thighs. "Your jeans are wet."

"I know. I'm going to take them off."

"Yeah?"

"Yeah. And then I'm gonna get into bed, cos it's freezing. I, uh, I think you should do the same."

"I'm not wearing jeans."

"Very funny." Paolo chanced a quick kiss to Luis's temple. It was the first time he'd pressed his lips to him in what felt like years, and the heat of it went straight to his dick. He backed out of Luis's grip and turned away, hiding it, as he stripped out of his jeans and the rest of his clothes.

Behind him, Luis was quiet and still, but Paolo felt his eyes boring into his back, and it only made his dick harder. He moved to the chest of drawers and found clean underwear and a T-shirt.

"Don't."

"Hmm?" Paolo glanced over his shoulder. "Don't what?"

Suddenly, Luis was beside him.

He took the underwear from Paolo's hand and put it back in the drawer. "Don't get dressed."

"Why not?"

In answer, Luis kissed him, sweeping him into his rain-damp arms and hot lips with enough force to send Paolo stumbling sideways. But he didn't fall. Luis held him firm and kissed him, and kissed him, and kissed him.

Stunned, Paolo let it happen, then, as the heat between them rose, he kissed Luis back like a starving man. He reclaimed his balance and let his hands roam free, searching for the warm skin he'd missed so much. But all he found were wet clothes. *Too many* clothes. He yanked Luis's T-shirt up his body, breaking their kiss only to wrench it over his head.

Luis's skin was cold but still as alluring as Paolo remembered it. More. He rubbed his palms over every inch he could reach, abs, chest, the wide expanse of Luis's back. Then he slid his fingers into Luis's overlong hair, tangling and twisting, as his cock strained against Luis's soggy sweatpants, desperately seeking friction.

The sweatpants had to go. Paolo pushed them over Luis's slim hips, taking his underwear for good measure. Luis's dick sprang free, and Paolo's mouth watered. But they'd sucked each other off a thousand times, and somewhere, deep within Paolo, a ghost screamed at him that it wasn't enough. Not this time. Not now.

He pulled back and pulled Luis's sweats all the way down to his ankles. "Get on the bed."

Luis obeyed and bent to pull his sweats and socks over his feet. When he straightened, his mouth was level with Paolo's dick. He licked his lips but made no move to take Paolo in his mouth, validating Paolo's instinct that their physical relationship had moved on. That Luis, that *both* of them, needed more.

Paolo pushed Luis back on the bed and covered him with his body. Their limbs entwined and melded together, and they kissed like liquid sex, grinding and thrusting, chasing the friction that made Paolo's eyes roll and his toes curl.

Luis's quiet moans set him on fire. He made a cradle

for himself between Luis's legs and slid his hand down his spine, cupping the rounded flesh he found there. "What do you want? Cos if we don't do something soon, I'm gonna come all over you without you ever touching my dick."

Eyes hooded, gaze hazed with heat, Luis bit his lip. "I want you."

"How?"

"However you're gonna give it to me."

His word choice gave Paolo pause. He'd imagined this moment a hundred times, mainly in the shower with his dick in his hand in the days after Luis had started work at the cafe, but before he'd found his way to Paolo's bed. In those fantasies, Luis had been the one on top, taking whatever pleasure he wanted with his dick buried deep, not on his back with his legs open and a shy smile.

Fuck. How is he even hotter than my dirty mind?

Paolo had no idea, and uncertainty didn't cut it. He gripped Luis's leg and bent it close to his chest, giving him better access. "Is that what you want? You want me to fuck you?"

"Yeah," Luis whispered. "I fucking dream about it."

Paolo's head spun at a million miles an hour. He kissed Luis hard, then softened it in a futile attempt to calm himself down. He wanted to ask Luis if he was sure, but something in Luis's gaze stopped him. Was it trust? Who the hell knew? But it was Luis's choice.

And he'd chosen Paolo.

He shifted up the bed, found lube and condoms in the bedside drawer, and tossed them on the pillow. Luis didn't look at them. He kept his eyes locked with Paolo's, but despite feeling closer to him than ever, the sense of him slipping away haunted the crazed desire surging through Paolo. He covered Luis again and gripped his chin. "Don't go."

Luis wrapped his legs around Paolo's waist. "I won't."

Paolo would never know if they were talking about the same thing. He drew back just enough to reach for a condom. He rolled it on and slicked himself with lube.

Luis swallowed.

Paolo kissed him. "Don't worry. I'll be gentle."

Luis made a low noise in the back of his throat, half growl, half whimper, but he said nothing. Just arched his body to meet Paolo, and Paolo took the hint.

He rubbed the excess lube on his fingers into Luis, probing, testing. Luis circled his hips and jacked himself, bottom lip caught between his teeth. His eyes fell closed, and a full-body shudder rocked him as Paolo slipped a finger inside him.

They'd done this before, more than once, and Paolo knew how to make Luis squirm, but as hot as that was, he was aching to move on. To slide inside Luis's tight body and fuck him until they came together.

Dizzy with want, Paolo reclaimed his fingers and snagged a pillow from the top of the bed. He slid it under Luis's hips, and bent his other leg to his chest. It wasn't a position he'd ever imagined Luis in, but *god*, he was so fucking hot. Paolo hunched over him and let his dick edge naturally to where he needed to be. Luis's tight muscle resisted him, but Paolo was in it for the long game. He moved slow, kissing every groan and gasp from Luis's lips until he was all the way in. Then he waited, stroking Luis's hair back from his sweaty face. "All right?"

Luis trembled. "Think so."

Paolo sat back on his heels, buried balls deep in Luis's tight body. He stared, transfixed, where they were joined, and slowly thrust his hips. A groan escaped him, and Luis moaned too.

"Fuck, do that again."

Paolo thrust again, harder this time but steady, and took up a grinding rhythm that dug pleasure out of Luis with the slow drive of his dick.

The pleasure was insane. Being naked with Luis had always made him feel like a pressure cooker about to blow, but fucking him was something else. Something precious, just like Luis.

Paolo became the sum of his sweat and moans, of the deep, searching thrust of his cock inside Luis. He fell forwards. Luis wrapped his legs around him like a vice. Paolo fucked him harder, and Luis writhed beneath him, a beautiful flush darkening his bare skin.

They kissed, tenderness forgotten in a mess of frantic lips and clashing teeth. Crushing warmth uncoiled in Paolo's gut, unloading more heat than he could handle. He dug his fingers into Luis's hips, his chest, his rigid biceps, and fought the inevitable. "Fuck, I'm gonna come."

Luis arched his back and drove up to meet Paolo's torturous thrusts. They met in the middle, over and over, pressed together with a hard desperation that forced the breath from Paolo's lungs. He reached for Luis's cock, but Luis was already there, jacking himself, eyes screwed shut.

Paolo gripped his chin. "Look at me. I wanna see you when you come."

Luis's eyes fluttered open, and the need swirling in them drew Paolo closer.

He fell forwards again, the change in angle driving him deeper. Madness overcame him, and every nerve seized up as he surged inside Luis. "Shit—"

Luis cried out, ragged and hoarse. "Fuck, I'm coming. Fuck."

He threw his head back, wet warmth spurting out of his dick, and clenched around Paolo so tight Paolo saw stars. Orgasm rippled through him, convulsing him, no inch of his body untouched. He was so fucking beautiful. Paolo watched him, entranced, but too soon, his own climax rushed him, and he shot deep and hard, his vision whiting out as he groaned loud enough to rattle the walls.

It seemed to go on forever. Paolo shuddered with after-shocks, and beneath him, Luis shivered, chest heaving.

Paolo let his dick ease from Luis's body. Luis made a soft sound that wasn't all pleasure. Paolo moved to roll away, but Luis caught him.

"Don't. Not yet."

He pulled Paolo down for a sticky, consuming kiss, and Paolo forgot about the condom he needed to bin, the mess of come and sweat between them, and the fact that Luis had double locked the front door the moment it had shut behind him. He forgot about everything except how it felt to lie naked with Luis, breathless and awed, as they kissed until Paolo was hard again.

The urge to fuck Luis again was so strong it almost blinded him to the fact that Luis was halfway to sleep, but as he gazed at Luis, the ache in his dick was easy to ignore. He pushed Luis's damp hair away from his face and stroked his scruffy jaw. Luis sighed, and it was as peaceful as Paolo had ever seen him.

Paolo ditched the condom, hustled him under the covers, and turned the lamp off. Luis pulled him close, burying his face in Paolo's neck, and immediately knocked out. It was cute as fuck, but sleep didn't find Paolo for a long time. For hours, he switched between gazing at Luis and staring at the ceiling. Convinced he'd see the dawn, he turned his alarm off, but eventually, he fell asleep.

It was light when he woke, and he knew without looking that he was alone. He opened his eyes to an empty bed. Luis was gone, leaving only rumpled sheets, his borrowed phone, and two full beer cans to show he'd been there at all.

20

Luis waited outside the industrial unit, his back to the lashing rain, transfixed by the crumpled photograph of Paolo's grandmother's nursing home. It had come through Paolo's door in the early hours of the morning. Luis had found it on a stumbling trip to the bathroom and had returned to bed to find it had been sent to his phone too from yet another unknown number.

A burner, no doubt, but the message was clear. Dante knew Luis had lied, and there was nothing he wouldn't do to punish Paolo if Luis didn't come through for him on this job.

Yeah? And then what? You think you'll do this for him and that'll be it? That he'll let you go?

Of course he wouldn't. But Luis didn't give a shit anymore. He'd spend the rest of his life muling rock if it kept Paolo safe. He stared at the grainy picture again, as if he needed reminding what was at stake, that his own pain was nothing compared to how Paolo would feel if something happened to Nonna.

Something that would be Luis's fault for being so fucking weak. *"Come home with me . . . please?"*

Hazy memories of what had come next haunted Luis in the best and worst ways. His body was wonderfully sore, but his heart ached so fierce he could hardly breathe. *You should've said no. Then you'd never have known what you'd lost.*

But that wasn't true. Even without the mind-blowing sex, Luis had left a piece of himself with Paolo that he'd never get back.

The door to the unit started to open, drawing Luis from his maudlin thoughts. On alert, he braced himself, waiting for Dante's contact to emerge. Years ago, it had been Fat Mo from the meat market, but life had moved on since then, and Luis had zero clue who was coming.

He kept to the shadows, watching and waiting. But instead of a person, a nondescript estate car emerged with Dante at the wheel. The car pulled up to where Luis loitered, and Dante opened the window. "Get in, brother."

Luis scowled. "You never said you'd be here."

"You didn't ask."

Truth. Based on past experience, Luis had assumed Dante would steer clear of his scuzz work, leaving the risk to anyone and everyone except himself. In fact, the only positive to his dawn appointment with a package of coke had been the certainty that Dante wouldn't be there. *Fuck my life.*

Luis got in the car. "Where did you find this heap of shit?"

Dante gunned the engine and peeled out of the industrial estate under the mist of the early morning. "Gumtree five years ago. I've been saving it for a job like this."

"Why? You told me to get the train. Besides, I haven't driven in years. I don't even know where my licence is. If I get pulled, they'll clock me for sure."

"Who said you were driving?"

Luis scowled. "No one. But as there's no one else here and you're too precious for the street, I made an assumption."

"Well, you know what they say about assumption."

"Actually, I don't. Explain it to me."

Dante drove out of the city and settled into the parade of trucks and lorries already on the road. "You said I didn't have the balls to come with you."

"So? That's always been true. You don't do jack to make your money 'cept play with people."

"What's wrong with that? The result is the same."

"You're a piece of shit, and you know it."

"If you say so, brother."

"Call me that again and I'll throw you out of this damn fucking car."

"Do it. You think I haven't got peeps outside your boy's house, waiting for my word if you fuck with me?"

Violent hate sluiced through Luis, malignant and sharp, eviscerating any emotion that had come before it. He eyed the oncoming traffic. It would be so easy to grab the wheel and steer the car into the path of the speeding

HGVs. It would kill him too, but if it kept Paolo safe, who the fuck cared?

Luis's hands twitched. Only the fear of hurting an innocent trucker kept him still. He had enough blood on his conscience.

The road to Coventry was clear. Two hours later, they crossed into the city. Luis kept track of landmarks, re-planning escape routes now their method of transport had changed, but as hard as he tried to keep his head in the game, his mind kept drifting to Paolo and the wrench of pain he still felt at leaving him behind.

Luis had slept with other men and spent the night in their beds, but he'd never been so consumed by someone, so fixated on every little thing about them. Paolo slept like a dead man, so he often didn't notice Luis creeping on him at night, counting his breaths, and playing with his soft, dark curls. Luis had always loved that about him, but he resented it now, for robbing him of the chance to see Paolo smile one last time. Cos Lord knew, he was going to be fucking fuming when he woke up to find Luis had bailed on him for good.

You don't deserve his anger. You don't deserve anything from him.

But God, Luis loved him . . . loved him so much he'd almost blurted it out in the park, and again when Paolo had fucked him so sweetly Luis had been close to tears with the pleasure. Luis could still feel it now, the profound heat, the wonder, the love. And the grief at letting it go. He fought to regain the numbness that had carried him through recovering from a beatdown with a metal pipe and six long years of the same four walls. Dug deep for it, scraping the pit of his soul.

The very worst of himself wasn't that hard to find, but the apathy was more elusive.

Dante said something.

Luis blinked at him. "What?"

"Nothing. Doesn't matter."

They drove on into the city. There was a big furniture store close to the motorway. Dante pulled into a space at the very back of the car park and shut the engine off. "We walk from here."

"Walk where?"

"A mile that way, to the house by the train station."

"Where's the package?"

"Under your seat."

Of course it was. Luis should've guessed that it would've been on him if they'd been stopped on route. That it was *still* on him, even now. "You haven't even touched it, have you? There's some kid's prints all over it instead of yours."

"Stop bitching and saddle up."

Luis sensed the shift in Dante's mood, and finally, the man who watched daytime TV in his underwear faded away, leaving behind the hard-faced bully who'd ruled Luis's life for as long as Luis could remember. Manipulative and cold, Dante was everything Luis despised, and hate bubbled in his chest again.

He rummaged under the seat and fished out a tape wrapped package. It was bigger than he'd expected, enough to score him another six years in the box. He held it out to Dante.

Dante smirked. "What do you think?"

"I think you're a pussyhole," Luis growled. "If you want me to carry this shit, you gotta give me your coat."

He'd never been more thankful that he'd left everything Paolo had ever given him behind—the phone, the hoodie. Dante took his coat off and handed it over. Luis put it on and gagged. "You smell like a wet dog."

"Whatever. Let's go."

They'd left the wet weather in London. Grey skies remained but without the wind and pelting rain. Dante checked the maps app on his phone and pointed west. "It's that way."

Luis rolled his eyes. "Seriously? You tapped the address into your phone? You're fucking green, man. No wonder you never rolled on the street."

Goading Dante was almost as stupid as a bullshit plan to mule drugs on foot through a retail park, but here they were. They followed the direction on Dante's phone and braved the underpasses crowded with tents and sleeping bags—the homeless not yet ready to face the day.

Luis wasn't ready either, but events had overtaken him.

The route Dante had mapped out hadn't taken account for the fact that they were on foot. Half a mile into their trek, they came to the busy A road.

"We have to cross it," Dante said.

Luis shot him a dark look. "You want to jaywalk across a dual carriageway at rush hour? Fuck it, we might as well do it naked if we're trying to draw attention to ourselves."

"Don't you think you've been naked enough recently?"

Luis's hands itched to close around Dante's throat. He stepped up, pressing his forehead to Dante's, forcing him to stumble towards the oncoming traffic. "Say that shit again, I'll fucking kill you."

Dante held his stare for a brave moment, then sensibly backed off. "There's no bridge. We don't have a choice."

Story of my fucking life. Luis turned away from Dante and stomped along the roadside, scanning both directions for the safest place to cross. Dante had brought them to a suicidal bend, but a straight stretch was up ahead.

Keeping a sharp eye out for transport police, Luis dashed across the first carriageway to the central reservation without looking to see if Dante followed him. The southbound lane was busier, but perched between the two, dithering time was limited. A break came, and he ran again, not stopping until he slid into the ditch on the other side.

Wet mud mottled his jeans, and brambles scratched his skin. Ridiculousness struck him, and he laughed as he scrambled to his feet. *Maybe this isn't real. Maybe I'll wake up and it'll be one of those fucked-up dreams after a dope-smoke session.*

Only problem with that theory was that Luis didn't smoke anymore. He'd left the cigarettes he'd bought the day before unopened on Paolo's bedroom floor. They were probably in the bin by now, unless he'd upset Paolo enough for him to smoke them.

Don't flatter yourself. As if you're worth it.

Dante joined Luis in the ditch. Luis walked on without

looking his way. They had four fields to cross before they hit civilisation again, and the rain had finally caught up with them.

Eventually, they reached the train station. Still busy with morning commuters, it was easy to blend into the crowds, even covered in mud. And Luis was used to walking with his head down, hands in his pockets. Dante, not so much. He liked to be noticed, and he didn't know how to be inconspicuous.

"Stop looking at people," Luis growled. "You want them to remember you?"

"What?"

"Every fucker that walks past, you meet their eye. Don't."

Dante stared at him like he was a mutant. "You don't think peeps will notice us if we *both* look like serial killers?"

Luis made an effort to soften his features, but it was hard to dial down the murder when Dante was this close. "Whatever. Where's the house? I want to be done with this shit."

"It's not a house."

"You said it was."

"I lied. It's an underground snooker club."

"Why would you—you know what? Never mind. Just tell me where it is."

Dante shrugged and pointed across the road. "It's right there."

Luis swung his gaze to the boarded-up snooker hall on

the opposite side of the street. It was as big of a shithole as the neighbourhood they'd left behind. "For real?"

Dante moved to cross the street. "Said so, didn't I?"

Luis caught his arm. "Wait. We need to scope the place out first."

"Why?"

"Because only a dumbfuck wouldn't. How many times have we fucked people over on an exchange? You think we'd have got away with that if they'd planned a way out first?"

"This isn't *Platoon*, fam."

"It's not Waitrose either, and you made me do this with you for a reason. Cos you knew I was the only person who wouldn't walk into it blind. So either listen to me or take this food in there your own damn self."

Dante let Luis steer him down the road and into a nearby pharmacy, the only business on the street that didn't look like the resident crew's own real estate. They wound up by the over-the-counter hearing aids. Scowling, Luis turned his back on them and faced Dante. "The club is in the basement?"

"Yeah. They said the front door would be unlocked, so just go on in and head downstairs."

"That's it?"

"What else do you want? A formal invitation?"

"I want to know how we get out of there if it goes tits up. Is there a back door? A fire escape?"

"I don't know."

"Then you need to find out, cos we're not going in there unless you do."

"Never had you pegged as a pussy. Guess you really don't like it, eh?"

"If you say so." Luis eyed the snooker club through the shop window. "They're expecting me, right? Not you?"

"Yeah. And you're supposed to be alone."

"Have you met any of them in person?"

Dante snorted. "Course not. You think I'm stupid?"

"Yeah, I do. But whatever. They won't be looking out for you, so head round the back and have a look."

"No."

"Do it. Or I'm flushing this package down the drain."

"You wouldn't do that."

"Wouldn't I?"

"You wouldn't have before prison made you soft."

Luis hauled Dante out of the shop and down a nearby alleyway. He threw him against the wall and drove his fist into Dante's gut hard enough to send him spluttering to the ground. "Prison didn't make me soft. It taught me what was worth fighting for, and it isn't you. Stay here, I'll be back in a minute."

He left Dante on his knees and ducked back onto the main street. The snooker club was on the end of a row of attached premises. Luis circled around, keeping his head down as he assessed the access routes. There was no back door, but a fire escape exited at the side, straight onto the pavement. If they came out that way with full pockets, they'd have to do it quietly. At least, Luis would. He didn't give a shit about Dante.

In the alleyway, he found Dante on his feet, red faced and irritated. "You gotta stop hitting me."

Luis grunted and pointed at the snooker club. "There's a fire door on the side. If we need to dip, we'll head for it and hope it's not locked."

"So dramatic."

"Whatever. Let's go."

Without waiting for Dante, Luis exited the alleyway and crossed the road. He strode straight to the boarded-up door, eased it open, and slipped inside.

Dante followed, his trademark blandness plastered back in place, and pushed past Luis towards the steep stairs that apparently led to the basement.

Luis trudged after him, keeping a sharp eye out for locked doors, cameras, and anything he could use as a weapon if things got real. A metal pipe caught his attention. He shuddered and looked away. He'd die before he picked it up.

At the bottom of the stairs, they met a reinforced door that was far newer than anything else in the building. Cameras guarded the shadowy entrance. Luis had learned long ago that hesitation gave away nerves to whoever was watching the camera feed. He knocked, hard and loud, and stepped back to give whoever was coming room to stare him down.

He didn't hear them coming until the door started to move, opening with a slow slide that revealed a man that made Asa look small. Large hands reached out, grabbed Luis's borrowed coat, and yanked him over the threshold, then Dante, and the door slammed shut behind them.

Irritated, Luis shook the hands off him. "The fuck? Where's your damn manners?"

The beefcake ignored him and stepped away, returning to the shadows. Luis got his bearings and glanced around the smoky room that was straight off the set of a Guy Richie film. Eastern European men sat around a table, drinking vodka and playing cards. There was even a parrot in a cage in the corner.

Show no fear. The package, pressed against Luis's ribs, seemed to throb. He squared his shoulders and fixed his stare at the man he pegged to be on top. "Got a delivery for you. Show me the paperwork."

The man jerked his head at the card table. "Show us the product first."

Same script, different day. Luis fished the brick from Dante's coat pocket and handed it over. Some of the weight in his chest lifted, as if his subconscious truly believed getting rid of the package brought him any closer to redemption.

Top boy took the brick to the table and slit it open with a flick knife he drew from his pocket while the big man stepped forward to check the rest of Luis's pockets. They came up empty, and beef cake moved on, but before he could lay his hands on Dante, the door behind burst open.

Masked men swarmed in, brandishing bats and knuckle dusters. Luis flattened himself against the nearest wall, but the men ignored him and surrounded the resident crew.

"Empty the safe," one of them growled.

Luis's damaged ear strained to catch the words, let alone identify the voice, but he'd always been good at remembering a profile. He studied the man's long neck and wiry shoulders. *Jesus fuck. It's Martell.*

He turned to Dante and was met with a smirk. *He set this up.* Of course. It made perfect sense. Why would Dante have wanted to come on a grunt mission? He never had before and was notorious for showing up after the fact, claiming glory for hustles he'd risked nothing to achieve.

Luis glared at him, fists bunched, ready to fly, but before he could move, the top boy with the flick knife drew a gun, and Luis didn't know whether to laugh or cry.

————

Silence reigned.

Time was contradictory. It passed in a flash, but events played out in slow motion, gunmetal glinting in the dimly lit room. It wasn't the first time Luis had seen a gun. He'd held them before. Carried them, fool that he'd been, with no real clue of how they worked. But, like everything, it had been years, and that period of his life belonged to someone else.

The man with the gun laughed. He pointed it at Martell and pulled back the safety. For the longest moment, Luis cringed, waiting for him to shoot, but at the last second, he swung left and fired directly into Dante's foot.

Dante screamed. And even with the fitted silencer, the shot rang out, reverberating around the underground room. Luis's weak ear popped. Splitting pain cracked through his skull. He clutched his head and ducked down, braced for all hell to break loose, but nothing happened. Martell's crew lowered their weapons without fear. Martell took his mask off, stance relaxed, and . . . he laughed.

From the floor, Dante moaned and flailed around his shattered foot. "Kill them," he gasped out. "And get me the fuck out of here."

Martell didn't look at him. He stepped forwards and reclaimed the brick of coke from the card table, then held out his hand to the grinning man with the gun. "I'll set up the real supply tonight. You good with the price?"

"We are."

"And you made it right with the St. Michael's boys?"

"Of course. Money talks, young one, and we have plenty of it."

Martell nodded. "I'll be in touch."

His crew filed out. Martell watched them go, then dropped down to Dante's level. "That was a message, bro. Did you get it?"

"You fucking snake," Dante spat. "I'm gonna kill you for this."

"You and whose army? I set this deal up months before you even thought of it. No one round here even knows who you are, and you think they'd do business with you?"

"It's my supply. All the links, the contacts. All mine."

Martell tilted his head. "Are they? When was the last time you made a call? Handled a mule? You got lazy, D. And no one cares anymore. You're through."

He started to stand. Dante made a crazy grab for his arm and missed.

Martell straightened, and for the first time, seemed to

notice Luis. He tossed him the package and pointed at Dante. "Plant this on him and dump him somewhere. Do that for me and I'll consider us done."

"Done?"

"Yeah. I know you don't want to roll anymore, and I'm cool with that if you make things right with the trash."

Luis snorted. "I don't have the means to dump him anywhere. He ditched the car miles away."

"Even better. It was stolen. Leave him in it."

"That doesn't help me."

"I'm not trying to help you," Martell retorted. "I don't give two shits about the fucking Pope brothers or whatever. Just do what I've asked, before these guys finish what they started—"

He broke off as the big man who'd searched them suddenly cursed at the CCTV he was monitoring on an iPad.

"What is it?" Martell demanded.

"Police," the man said. "They come. Two minutes."

How the hell he knew that, Luis had no idea. *They must have cameras every fucking where.*

The room began to empty out through a door Luis hadn't clocked. It was concealed by a black curtain and somehow led to daylight.

Martell ghosted through it, leaving his bargain basement drugs behind.

In Luis's hand.

The rest of the room cleared, parrot and all, and panic hit Luis square in the gut. The police were coming, and he was holding enough coke to put him away long enough to have middle-aged spread by the time he got out. Add in that Dante had a bullet in him, and they were both royally fucked.

Run. If you leave now, you can get away. But as hard as Luis tried to make himself move, nothing happened, and it took him far too long to realise his treacherous heart wouldn't let him leave Dante alone and bleeding on the snooker club floor.

A shout ripped, unbidden, from Luis's chest. He punched the wall and wrenched Dante's coat off, flinging the sweaty leather away before he thought better of it and crouched to drape it over Dante's shivering form. "I fucking hate you."

Dante chuckled, flat and breathless. "I know. And I get it now, so you should go, now, before they get here."

"You know I won't leave you like this, so don't pretend to be a god damn martyr now."

"I'm not. I mean it. Leave the package and get the fuck out of here. That way, you've given Martell what he wants and got rid of me all in one. You can't lose, brother."

Luis had been losing his entire life, ever since genes and DNA had gifted him Dante and their waster mother as his only family. Dante's words washed over him as he tracked the sound of the approaching sirens.

Dante gripped his arm, fingers digging in hard. "Fuck's sake, Luis. Just *go.* I'm fucked anyway, and you don't deserve to get caught here."

"I can't—"

"You can. Just like I left you all those years ago. Get the fuck out of here."

Dante's blood was seeping into Luis's jeans and the hem of Paolo's sweater. He was in no danger of dying, but the sight of it made Luis's stomach roll and his heart clench with fear. The more blood he had on him, the more conspicuous he became. If he was going to run, it had to be now.

"I—"

Dante shook his head. "Don't. Leave me here and I'll get help quicker. Go, Luis. Now. *Run.*"

Luis backed up and staggered to his feet. Blue lights were already visible through the escape door the others had left open, narrowing his options to the front or the fire door on the side, if he could even find it.

With one last look at Dante, he turned and fled into the dark club, chasing an instinct that led him past a defunct bar and into what looked like a storeroom. He tripped over an empty box. In the gloom, he threw out a hand, and it hit the cool metal bar of a fire door. *This is it.* Luis listened hard for the sound of footsteps behind him, but even with adrenaline-sharp senses, he heard nothing but the roar of his own heart.

Fuck it.

He pushed the bar down.

The door opened with a whiny screech that reached even Luis's ears. He cringed, bracing himself, and squinted into the daylight. The door had opened onto the bustling pavement. He stuck his head out, glanced swiftly in both directions, then melted into the crowd, head down, hood up. He followed the flow, jaw clenched, gaze darting, steeling himself for a heavy hand on his shoulder. To be tackled to the ground and cuffed.

But it didn't happen. He walked and walked and walked until he found himself alone in a city that wasn't his home without a clue what to do next.

21

Luis had been gone, *again*, for less than a day by the time Paolo lost his shit and went looking for him. The recurring theme of him banging on unanswered doors with no fucking clue was driving him up the wall, but somehow, he couldn't bring himself to stop. Maybe if they hadn't fucked, it would've been easier. But they had fucked, and it had been the final puzzle piece that now tied Paolo's soul so entirely to a man who came with a camel's back of baggage.

He had no regrets, though. Just a razor-sharp fear that wouldn't fade until he knew for sure that Luis was okay.

There was no answer at the bedsit. Paolo wandered the nearby streets for an hour, hoping that Luis would appear, as he so often did, around the next corner, but eventually, he gave up and returned to the bedsit to wait.

The exterior door was still broken. Paolo slipped into the old house and felt his way back to Luis's door. He knocked again for good measure, but there was still no reply.

Luis's front door was made from the cheapest wood and secured by a lock that looked like it had come from the Argos catalogue. Paolo was no gangster, but he knew the credit card trick as well as any face from the neighbourhood. He slid his maxed out Mastercard between the doorframe and the lock and forced the lock back into the door with a quiet click. The door swung open a half inch. Paolo pushed it the rest of the way and quickly flicked the lights. "Anyone home?"

No reply came, but with Luis's damaged hearing, silence didn't mean much. Paolo shut the door behind him and listened for signs of life. There were none. He ventured further inside and found the bedsit as empty as Luis's fridge.

Defeated, Paolo sank down onto Luis's meticulously made bed, then jumped back up and turned the lights off to preserve Luis's electric tokens. Darkness swamped him, in more ways than one, and he shivered against the draughty chill of the bedsit. *Jesus. How does he live here?*

It was a rhetorical question, but the answer came to Paolo all the same. *Because he has to. Without Toni and Nonna, where would you be?*

Paolo wrapped his arms around himself, tipped his head back against the wall, and chased the bliss he'd found with Luis less than twenty-four hours before, when he'd been buried deep inside him and Luis had whispered sweet, desperate pleas in his ear. Paolo had never fucked anyone like that. Had never been so consumed by pleasure and emotion that, when it was over, he could barely remember the details, only how it had felt. How it *still* felt. His body thrummed with too many feelings to catch, but most of all, it was awe and wonder. Luis was so fucking beautiful he made Paolo's soul ache. *I miss him.*

He closed his eyes.

Somehow, he dozed off, not entirely asleep, but not conscious either.

The squeak of the front door roused him sometime later. Dazed, Paolo lurched off the bed and staggered to the hallway just as Luis stumbled inside. Paolo's eyes were already adjusted to the darkness. He edged forwards, arms outstretched. "Luis?"

Luis jumped. His head jerked up like a puppet and his tortured gaze dragged in the shadows until it landed on Paolo. He blinked hard, started forwards, then stopped and shook his head hard enough to give himself a seizure.

Alarmed, Paolo closed the distance between them and pulled Luis fully into the flat, letting the door slam shut behind him. "Jesus. What's the matter?"

Luis stared, intense and yet somehow distant. His eyes darted between Paolo's face, and his hands gripping Luis's wrists. "You're not here. You can't be here."

"Of course I'm here. I was worried about you."

"No. You can't be. You were never real."

"I was," Paolo whispered. "I *am*. I promise."

Luis took a breath as if to speak, but no sound came out. His eyes rolled back, and despite Paolo's hold on him, he fell to the floor.

Paolo had always hated the sight of blood. Childhood nosebleeds had often sent him to the deck, and when it happened, Toni had always carried him to bed and left him to wake up on his own. Nonna? Not so much. Paolo couldn't count the number of times she'd panicked and chucked cold water in his face.

He'd never understood it. Not until now as he held Luis in his arms and willed him to wake up. "Come on, come on." He pushed Luis's wet hair back from his face. "Come on."

It felt like a year, but in reality, barely a few seconds had passed when Luis's eyes fluttered open. For a long moment, his gaze was empty and disoriented, then he zeroed in on Paolo and sat up sharply. "What the fuck?"

Paolo withdrew, giving him room. "You fainted, I think. Unless you're drunk, but I can't smell booze on you."

Luis shook his head, slower this time, without giving them both whiplash. "I'm not drunk."

"Okay." Paolo edged closer. "You want to tell me what's up then? Cos you look like you've just found a dead body."

Luis blanched. "Don't joke about that shit."

"Then tell me the truth."

Luis leaned against the door behind him, still pale and looking like a man about to hurl his guts.

Paolo got up and fetched water from the kitchen. Luis took it with hands shakier than Paolo had ever seen and drank it down in one gulp.

"You want more?" Paolo asked.

"No."

"Anything else you need?"

"No."

"Then speak."

"Why?"

"Why do you think?" Paolo's patience snapped, and his shout rang out in the dark bedsit. "Because you ran out on me *again*, and you've come back looking like you've fucking died twice already, and Jesus fucking Christ, is that blood on your clothes?"

Luis's gaze flickered to the ominous stains on his jeans. "Do you really want the truth? Cos if I tell you, I can't take it back."

"Is it worse than the shit you've already told me?"

"I don't think so, not for me, at least. But it could be if the police find out."

"Did you hurt someone?"

"No."

"You promise?"

Luis snorted out a humourless laugh. "Is that all you're afraid of?"

"Not even close. If you knew everything I was afraid of, your brain would explode."

"It already did." Luis tapped the scar on the side of his head. "But we've done that story already."

"Actually, we haven't. You told me you got hit with a bar and it was Dante's fault. You never said why."

"I don't know why."

"For real?"

"For real. It was a beef I didn't know about until after."

They were getting off track. Maybe one day, Paolo would want to know every little thing that had shaped Luis into the man Paolo loved, but right now, only the last twenty-four hours mattered.

Paolo helped Luis up and guided him to his bed. He sat him down and fetched more water.

Luis waved it away. Paolo set the glass on the windowsill and pointed to Luis's stained clothes. "Take them off. I'll put them in the wash."

"You don't have to do that."

"Take them *off*."

Luis stood, pulled his T-shirt over his head, and unbuttoned his jeans.

Paolo tried not to stare as the jeans slid lower and lower, but god, it was hard. Even dishevelled, dirty, and deflective, Luis was insanely attractive. *I wish fucking him would make it all go away*. But as the errant thought crossed his mind, he nixed it. Sex wasn't a substitute for honesty, and it never would be. He needed the truth, and he needed it now.

He took Luis's clothes to the washing machine and set the load to wash on the hottest cycle. The machine whirred to life, and Paolo watched, lost, as it filled with water. Luis called to him like a siren, but Paolo was drowning. *Whatever he tells me, I won't know what to do. I can't—*

Cool arms slid around Paolo's waist. He gasped, shock rippling through him as Luis melded to his body from behind, pressing his naked form against Paolo's coat and rough jeans.

"I'm sorry," he whispered. "I'm sorry I keep doing this to you."

Paolo gritted his teeth. "Doing what? I don't even know what's happened."

"I know."

Luis pressed harder against Paolo, the sharp lines of his body, from his shoulders to his abs and strong thighs, digging into Paolo's flesh, warming him with the molten promise of fire. Paolo closed his eyes and leaned into the pleasure, the heat of Luis's body going straight to his dick, clouding his brain. *No.* He shook his head to clear it, but his cock hardened all the same, and fresh anger surged through him, at himself as much as Luis.

He spun around, pushing Luis away. "Don't."

"Don't what?" Luis said flatly. "Touch you?"

"As if I don't want you to touch me."

"Then what do you want? Me to spill my guts a thousand times until you finally realise I'm not worth all the bullshit I bring to the table?"

"Yeah, it's that fucking easy."

Paolo made for the door, but Luis caught his arm and dragged him back. "Then let it happen."

"Let *what* happen?"

Luis pulled Paolo close enough to palm the bulge in Paolo's jeans. "This. I know you want me, and you have to know how much I want you too."

Of course Paolo knew. Luis's rock-hard dick was hard to miss, and . . . impossible to ignore. He let Luis draw them together, and his hands found their way to Luis's hips, sealing the deal until they were pressed against each other so tight Paolo shuddered and sank his teeth into Luis's neck.

Luis groaned and arched, offering Paolo more of his neck.

Paolo bit deeper and sucked, tasting blood, as Luis writhed against him. Desire made him blind. He unbuckled his belt and half freed his aching dick before rational thought abruptly returned, and he pushed Luis away a second time. "No. This can't happen. Not now."

He took his chance and escaped from the bathroom.

Luis followed him into the kitchen and tugged him away from the window. He eased Paolo's coat off his shoulders and let it fall to the ground. "I know it's the wrong thing for us to do right now, that you need so much more from me, but I can't do anything else . . . not yet. Please. I need you."

"I'm not going to rage bang you when you just passed out."

"I didn't pass out."

"You really did."

"Please."

Paolo squeezed his eyes shut, scrabbling for strength he didn't possess. Luis whispered his plea again, plaintive, desperate, and Paolo's resolve crumbled to dust.

He opened his eyes and pointed at the bed. "Fine. Have it your way. Get on your damn knees."

22

Luis had never been more thankful that past him—the one who'd oh-so-briefly believed getting naked with Paolo could be a long-term thing—had optimistically bought a bottle of lube and stashed it in the bathroom.

He waited on the bed while Paolo fetched it.

Paolo came back, spinning it in his hands, his expression hungry and grim. "No condoms."

"We don't need them. I got tested, like, five years ago, and I've only been with you."

"You got tested in prison?"

"Yeah. They offer it to all queer inmates."

"I got done a month before you got out."

Luis nodded, not asking why because he didn't want the answer. He didn't want anything except Paolo.

His dick throbbed with need. He rose up on his knees, weak with fatigue and hunger but unable to contemplate anything but Paolo. He held out his hand. "Come here . . . please?"

Paolo knocked his hand away. "Stop saying that."

"What?"

"Stop saying *please*. It makes me crazy."

"Crazy how?"

"Crazy like I want to bend you over and fuck your brains out."

Finally, they were getting somewhere. Luis licked his lips. "Do it."

"Are you sure?"

"Yeah. Fuck me. I need it."

Paolo groaned, and something seemed to give inside him. He shoved Luis's chest and turned him around, pushing him down onto the mattress. Adrenaline sparked in Luis's tired veins. He widened his legs and shivered as he heard Paolo shuck his jeans. Rough hands—perfect hands—shifted Luis around until he was where Paolo wanted him, hips raised, legs spread, lube dripping down his thighs.

Luis was dizzy with need. He hung his head, shoulders quivering, and shouted out a deep groan as Paolo entered him. The stinging burn was everything. He was still sore from the first time, but he pushed back on Paolo's dick, craving more. "More."

Paolo grunted and slid all the way in, his bare cock filling Luis to the brim. For a protracted few seconds, he stayed stone still, as if frozen in place. Then he growled and gave Luis what he wanted, snapping his hips back and slamming into Luis hard enough to make the bed jump.

Luis cried out. It hurt, but he liked it. Clung to it, as though the pound of Paolo's cock inside him could erase the day and bring him back to earth. Pain gave way to dark pleasure. Sounds he didn't recognise fell from him, and he arched his spine, responding to Paolo's bruising grip. "Harder, harder."

Paolo growled and fucked him harder, hunching over Luis's back, gripping Luis's shoulders, his strained moans like god damn poetry. Skin slapped skin, and Luis was flying, lost to the coil of pleasure unravelling in his belly. He reached for his cock, but for the second time in the space of ten minutes, Paolo knocked his hands away.

"No. You want this, you let me give it to you."

Luis had never come hands free. He'd seen it in porn, but always figured it was Viagra induced or another magic trick, not something that happened between ordinary men. But there was nothing ordinary about the electrifying climax that barrelled towards him as Paolo drilled him. It touched every part of him, clenching his fists and curling his toes. He shouted again, chasing it, and yet somehow afraid of it. "Fuck, I'm gonna come. I'm gonna come so fucking hard."

Paolo's rhythm grew more frantic, and his cock swelled and pulsed inside Luis. His groans turned desperate, tipping Luis over the edge as orgasm hit, Luis first, then Paolo.

With a ragged yell, Luis drove his fist into the mattress, spilling his release over the duvet cover, thighs quivering, equilibrium lost, if he'd ever even had it, all while Paolo kept fucking him.

His cock dragged over Luis's prostate. It was the best kind of torture. Coming seemed to last forever, but of course it didn't. Growling, Paolo drove in deep and stayed there, juddering as he came too, tying them together as Luis trembled with aftershocks.

And then it was over. Luis fell slack, and Paolo slid out of him with far more care than he'd entered. He disappeared, but not for long. He came back with a warm, wet towel—Luis's only towel—and cleaned them both up.

Luis rolled onto his back, exhaustion settling into his bones. His eyes were heavy with the sleep he so desperately needed, but as Paolo returned to the bed again, he knew their strangest of nights was far from over. "Are you going to tell me how you got into my place without a key?"

Paolo shrugged and sat on the edge of the bed, naked from the waist down but still wearing his T-shirt. "I wasn't always a good boy, and your door is rubbish."

Luis couldn't argue with that, and he yearned to know more about what had happened in Paolo's life to teach him how to break and enter, but he'd run out of time for deflection. He owed Paolo an explanation. More than that, he owed him the truth.

He coaxed Paolo into his bed, and in the dark bedsit, lit only by the slivers of streetlight from outside, told him everything, right up until the moment he'd left Dante bleeding on the sticky snooker club floor.

Paolo listened in silence, his expression unreadable, but his wandering fingertips held Luis's fear at bay. "So you left the drugs with Dante? Like that Martell dude wanted you to?"

"Yeah."

"Was it hard to leave your brother?"

Luis nodded. "Annoyingly so, even though it was his fault I was there at all."

"You'll probably feel guilty about it for a while."

"You think?"

"For sure. That's where you're totally different to him, right?"

"I don't know."

"Well, you should. And I guess you need to live with that guilt for as long as it's there. Fighting it won't change anything."

"You're so wise."

Paolo hummed and slid further down the bed. "Not really. If I was, I probably wouldn't have broken into a road boy's flat."

"Ex road boy."

"No offence, mate, but I've heard that shit before."

"And it was true when I said it. I only went with Dante because—" Luis stopped. He'd promised Paolo the truth, but was he really about to tell him Dante had been creeping on his elderly grandparents? Holy fuck, his life was a mess.

"Because what?" Paolo nudged him. "And don't give me bullshit. I gave *you* what you needed, now it's my turn."

Luis's sore body still tingled from Paolo turning him inside out. He shivered a little, but not from cold. "Dante threatened you. Said he'd fuck up you and your family if I didn't do what he wanted. So . . . I did."

Paolo's dancing fingers stilled. "You went on a drugs run to Coventry to protect me?"

Luis shrugged, glad Paolo hadn't swooped on the entire

truth. "Of course. I promised you—and myself—that Dante's drama wouldn't ruin your life too. Maybe I should've looked closer at what he was doing, talked more with Asa and Martell before I took him seriously, but I've been out of the game a long time, man. I thought he was still a king."

Paolo said nothing. Just resumed his attentions to Luis's forearms, a deep frown creasing his forehead.

Luis rolled onto his side and smoothed the line away. "What are you thinking?"

"Lots of things."

"Like?"

"Like how you should've had a better way to deal with your brother's manipulation than committing a crime, but I'm starting to understand why you didn't."

"You are?"

"Kind of. You can't choose your family, can you? I get that, trust me."

"I do trust you."

Paolo smiled a little. "I know. And maybe when the dust has settled from this, I'll trust you too."

His words hurt, but Luis understood them. Paolo had always been brutally honest with him. It was why Luis loved him. And, fuck, did he love him. So much. "I don't know what I would've done if you hadn't been here when I got back."

"I wasn't sure you were coming back."

"How long were you going to wait?"

Paolo flushed. "Well, I told myself I'd wait forever, but I

guess I'd have had to give up eventually. That greasy spoon doesn't run itself."

A light bubble of laughter warmed Luis's chest, but Paolo remained serious.

"We need to figure out what you're going to do," he said. "You don't know if you got in and out of that club unseen. The police could've been watching it all along."

"I thought of that. When I'd calmed down enough to think rationally, I went and sat outside the snooker club while they were clearing it out to see if they'd notice me. When they didn't, I sat outside the police station for an hour too."

"That's what you call rational thought?" Paolo whistled. "Though I suppose it was as good a plan as any if you actually wanted them to pick you up."

"I didn't want them to. It was more that if they were going to, I wanted it over and done with. Not to look over my shoulder for the next six months."

"Dante won't talk?"

"Nah. He'd get murdered in prison if he snitched."

"Fair enough. What about the cameras in the club?"

"I couldn't see how many there were, but it was pretty dark, and they were accessed remotely. I've never been lucky, but that changed when I met you, so who knows?"

"You met me when you were eleven, you just didn't notice."

Luis opened his mouth to voice his regret, but a hardcore yawn overwhelmed him, cracking his jaw.

Paolo took pity on him and rolled onto his back, tugging Luis to lie against him with his head on his chest.

He carded gentle fingers through Luis's hair. "Don't worry about it now, baby. We'll figure it all out."

He was tired too, and the intimate endearment seemed to fall from him with little conscious thought. But Luis heard it like he'd shouted it in his good ear, and he thought of nothing else until he fell asleep.

———

Luis woke to the promising light of the imminent spring. And to Paolo straddling him and sinking down on Luis's rigid cock. "*Fuck*."

Paolo gasped out a ragged laugh. "I was hoping you got the memo."

Luis's brain struggled to catch up with the race his body was already winning. He watched, spellbound, as Paolo ground down on him, pleasuring himself with his hand as he rode Luis's cock, screwing Luis with the satanic tilt and roll of his pelvis.

It was perfection.

Luis bent his legs to support Paolo's back.

Paolo moaned. "Yeah, that's it. Right there."

"Yeah? You like that? I thought you were a power top."

"That's funny. You thought I didn't bottom? Wow . . . fuck yeah, I do it all."

Paolo's incoherency set Luis on fire, and he questioned whether he was actually awake or whether a day on the road had gifted him the best dreams of his life. Either way, he was so here for Paolo's versatility. It suited Luis down to the ground. He'd never been able to choose what he liked best—getting dicked out or burying himself deep inside someone, searching for the trigger to make them blow.

And Paolo was going to blow, and suddenly nothing mattered except making that happen.

Luis thrust up, meeting Paolo in the middle. A flush darkened Paolo's olive skin, and another moan tore from his chest. "Do it," he whispered. "Make me come."

He started to fall apart, fucking himself deep on Luis's dick, and everything about him sent Luis crashing over the edge. A long, bone-deep orgasm ripped through him. He dug his fingers into Paolo's hips and thrust hard, chasing the pleasure that already had him frantic with need. His cock pulsed, and he filled Paolo, exulting in the sensation of Paolo clenching around his bare dick. It was like nothing he'd ever known, and a rare clarity struck him as hard as his climax: he didn't need pain to be a better man. He needed this, with Paolo, forever and always.

Still groaning, Paolo fell forwards. Luis caught him but couldn't stop fucking him, milking every drop of heat that flowed between them until sweat and shivers were all they had left.

He wrapped his arms tight around Paolo, ignoring the sticky mess between them. "I was worried it was your turn to run out on me. Never once did I picture you waking me up like *that*."

"Yeah, well, don't expect it every morning."

The implication that they had more mornings to spend together made Luis's soul sing. He squeezed Paolo impossibly tighter, then let him go. "The police might come looking for me today, even if they don't know I was there.

They have to tell someone he got hurt, or get my probation officer on the case."

"What about your mum?"

"He'd never give them her details. It's not how we do. What time is it?"

"Early. My alarm hasn't gone off yet. But I've been thinking about that."

"What? Your alarm?"

"No. About work. I think you should come with me and carry on like none of this ever happened, any of it, not just yesterday."

"You mean the weeks and weeks of my fuck-ups, not just this one?"

"Don't be a prick. I mean *all* of it, which includes my fuck-ups too, like pushing you out of your job in the first place."

"That's not what—"

Paolo clamped his hand over Luis's mouth. "Whatever. We can argue about that later. At work, where you'll have been all day after spending the night with me."

"You're not lying to the police for me."

"That's not what I'm suggesting. I just think it'll look better if it's business as usual. *Our* usual, not Dante's."

Paolo glared down at Luis before letting his hand slip away. Luis let his suggestion settle, turning it over in his mind. There was no way he was going to let Paolo tell the police he'd been with him all day yesterday or any other day he'd been elsewhere, but reclaiming his job at the cafe was more appealing than he could ever say. And Paolo's theory made sense. It was a normal day, right?

Whatever that meant. He nodded slowly. "Let's go to work."

They rose from their sex pit, showered, and dried off with the half of Luis's towel they hadn't cleaned up with the night before. Then they walked to work, side by side, hands brushing, and opened the cafe as if the last few weeks really hadn't happened. Luis cooked while Paolo served and cleaned up. It felt so right, Luis didn't know what to do with it, and if not for the two policemen who rocked up after lunch, he may well have believed it was nothing but a dream.

Paolo directed the coppers to the kitchen and took over the grill. "Be nice," he muttered. "They seem friendly enough."

"If you think that, then you don't know coppers." But Luis wiped his hands and plastered a friendly expression on his face all the same. If the night he'd spent with Paolo had taught him anything, it was that first times came when he least expected them.

He ducked into the kitchen. The policemen smiled in greeting. *Case in point.* "Afternoon, Mr Pope. Sorry to bother you at work, but I'm afraid we've got some not-so-pleasant news for you."

"Okay . . . " Luis frowned and leant against the counter. "Get it over with then."

"It's about your brother, Dante. He was injured by gunshot yesterday afternoon. Nothing life threatening, from what we understand, but he's still in the hospital with severe injuries to his foot."

"His foot?"

"Yes. It seems someone shot him there."

"Wow." Luis blew out a long breath. "Do you know what happened? I'm guessing it wasn't a hunting accident."

"Not quite. Do you have any idea where he was yesterday afternoon?"

"No. I make it my business not to know where he is."

"When did you last see him?

"A few days ago? A week maybe? I went to his flat in Moss Farm to pick up some stuff he kept for me there when I went inside."

"What kind of stuff?"

"Clothes. Music."

"Where did you take it?"

"Nowhere. He'd chucked it years ago."

"That was nice of him."

"He's a nice person."

A slight smirk graced the police officer's face. "So I've heard. On that note, I should tell you he's also under arrest for drug and firearm offences, for which he'll be interviewed as soon as he's fit to do so. When he's out of hospital, you should expect him to go straight on remand. I can't imagine a circumstance where he won't be charged."

"Give a shit."

"You're not close then?"

"Not since I did my bird and came out. I'm not about that road life anymore."

"I'd heard that too." The officer glanced around the kitchen. "Have you been working here long?"

"Since I got released."

"How often do you work?"

"Every day," Paolo said as he bustled in with a tray of dirty cups. "And he spends every night with me too, so tell that brother of his to do one."

The officer laughed. "I'm not planning on talking to Dante Pope anytime soon, but I take your point. It's nice for us to see an offender making a go of their life on the outside. That's all I meant."

Paolo scowled and left as abruptly as he'd arrived.

Luis shook his head. "Sorry. My boyfriend's Italian. There's no reasoning with him."

"I get that. My wife is the same." The officer closed his notebook and straightened up. "We won't take any more of your time, but if I may make one suggestion?"

"Go on."

"Your brother stands to go away for quite some time. That leaves a power vacuum in the Moss Farm towers. I'm sure you understand what I mean when I say it's a place you're best giving a wide berth for however long it takes things to settle."

"If you're asking me not to start a turf war with whatever idiot wants Dante's crown, trust me, I'm not interested."

"Glad to hear it. Take care, Mr Pope."

The police left via the back door. Luis shut it behind them. Locked it with steady hands, and felt another heft of weight shift from his shoulders. His chest moved freely, and green shoots of hope sprouted in his gut.

Paolo returned to the kitchen with more dishes. "Sorry, I didn't mean to be rude. It's just how I am."

Luis laughed loud enough that even he heard the joy in

it. Paolo looked startled. Luis lunged for him and swept him up in an embrace that drove the breath from both of them. "I love that you're rude, and I love *you*, so fucking much."

He swung Paolo around without waiting for his response, only setting him down when equilibrium deserted him.

Laughing, Paolo steadied them on the countertop and planted the mother of all kisses on Luis's lips before he pulled back with a shit eating grin. "That's a bit of luck, mate. Because I love you too, and I was kind of worried it was gonna be a problem."

"Really? You love me?"

"Course I do, you fool. I don't give my pasta secrets away to just anyone, you know."

"But you gave them to me?"

"I did. And I'd do it a hundred times more if you promise me one thing."

"Anything."

Paolo took Luis's face in his hands and took him hostage with his molten gaze. "Stop thinking you're not worth it, because you are. You're worth the fucking world to me, and it doesn't matter what other people do or say, nothing about that is ever going to change."

EPILOGUE

Six months later

Luis turned Paolo on his side, holding his leg up, and kept fucking him, entranced by the sounds Paolo made and the rippling tension in his beautiful back. Paolo didn't often let him fuck him like this. He liked to be in control, and Luis was happy to let him be, but in moments like this, when he wasn't, Luis couldn't get enough.

Paolo came, hunching his back and groaning into a pillow. Orgasm crashed into Luis too, and he shot hard, thrusting deep into Paolo until a final shudder rocked him.

He kissed Paolo's neck and let his dick slip free.

Paolo was wrecked. He lay boneless and still as Luis cleaned up around him, then let out a quiet laugh. "I never knew what fucked senseless meant until you. My brain is total cotton wool right now."

"I like you like that. Makes me feel clever."

"You are clever. I have a still-functioning dishwasher to

prove it. I'd have thrown that prick out of the window without you."

Luis didn't doubt it. The last six months had done nothing to mellow Paolo's fiery disposition, and even better? Luis now heard every rage-fuelled word that came out of his mouth. At least he did if he remembered to slip the tiny flesh-coloured aid into his ear canal when he woke up.

As if he'd read Luis's mind, Paolo opened the drawer and passed Luis the box, keeping his back turned while Luis fitted the device into his ear and shuddered as new sounds filtered into his brain, loud, and not all of them pleasant.

He tilted his head sideways and shook it. "I still don't like this thing. It feels funny."

Paolo rolled over. "They said it would feel strange for a little while, and it's only been two weeks."

"Since when are you the voice of reason?"

"Since you decided you weren't." Paolo rose up on his knees and beckoned Luis closer. He took his face in his hands and studied the ear where Luis had placed the device. "Look, I get that it feels weird and eating crunchy shit freaks you out, but give it a chance, okay? Wear it when we fuck, then you'll really know how loud I get when you—"

"If you're finishing that sentence, you're gonna be late for work."

Paolo shrugged. "The boss likes me."

Luis grumbled some more, and Paolo left him to it and sauntered off to the shower. Luis watched him go, caught up, as ever, in his lovely nakedness, but once the bathroom door shut, reality returned to him. He had shit to do today, and the sooner he got it done, the sooner he could go back to a world where Paolo being naked was the only thing that made his heart race.

———

Luis waited by the canal, watching the ducks fight over bread a toddler was throwing from the bridge. In the distance, the Moss Farm towers still blighted the horizon, but not for him. Dante had finally relinquished his penthouse lair back to the council, and a new family lived there now.

Footsteps sounded behind him. He turned sharply, still unused to hearing people coming.

Asa raised his hands. "Easy, Luis. How's tricks?"

"Not bad. I'd ask you the same, but I don't want to know."

"Probably not." Asa's grin was easy. "I'm guessing you want to know how it went yesterday, though?"

Luis shrugged.

Asa nodded and took a seat at the other end of the bench. "He got nine years and an order to stay out of the neighbourhood for life, so even when he gets out, he can't come back here. Community safety and all that."

"And yet you're still here."

"So are you, mate."

"What about Martell?"

Asa's gaze drifted to the grubby water. "He isn't around anymore."

"Since when?"

"Thought you didn't want to hear about my tricks?"

Luis conceded the point. He'd been vaguely aware of the power struggle the police had warned him about, but he'd had other things on his mind, and it had been all too easy to stay away. "You're right. I don't care about any of that. You know why I'm here."

"You want to know if I'm gonna call on you for work?"

Luis nodded. "I figured you'd left me alone because of the heat from Dante's case, but that's over now."

"So?"

"So . . ." Luis forced himself to look at Asa. "Just be real with me. I need to know."

"There isn't anything to know. Dante's gone, man. And he was the only one who wanted you back on the road. Me and Martell didn't agree on much, but we both knew you'd be a liability if you didn't want to be there, and that hasn't changed."

"What about the threats Dante made to the Cilberto family?"

Asa huffed out a laugh. "He did that shit on his own. Come on, Luis. Even if you didn't know me, you think stalking elderly folk is good for business?"

"I don't know you. It's been nearly seven years since we had a real conversation."

"We never had real conversations."

Another point to Asa, but Luis didn't care. Instinct had already predicted that Asa had zero interest in

Luis's life, and perhaps he'd been a fool to force an encounter that didn't need to happen, but it felt good to hear the words. And even better to know that he didn't have to go home and lie about where he'd been. He'd made Paolo a promise—no more secrets—and it proved easier to keep than he'd ever dared dream.

He left Asa by the water and walked into town for no other reason than he wanted to see Paolo. It was Monday, the quietest day of the week, and Paolo had taken to not letting Luis work, but there were no rules about visiting, a loophole Luis exploited on a regular basis.

The cafe was easing down from the breakfast rush as Luis slipped in the back door. Paolo was in the kitchen, slicing mushrooms and muttering under his breath about whichever poor soul had annoyed him. He glanced up as Luis shut the door, and his smile was all Luis would ever need.

Redemption? Nah. He just wanted to live.

———

Toni's thick brow furrowed as he glanced around the half-furnished flat. "It's nice, but I don't understand why you moved. There was nothing wrong with where you lived before."

Paolo sighed, searching for the patience only Luis seemed to possess when having this conversation for the dozenth time. "I already told you. It was weird to live in my flat while Luis worked for me too. It wasn't fair on him for me to have so much power over him, that's why we didn't move into the flat above the cafe either."

"I didn't hear him complaining."

"So? That didn't make it right."

Toni shook his head and moved on to inspect the kitchen, and Paolo tried not to regret bringing him out for the day, something he'd only had time to do since Nonna had passed away. Losing her had been harder than Paolo had ever feared, but life went on. And Toni seemed happy enough when he wasn't bitching about Paolo's housing decisions.

He took Toni back to the home after lunch, then returned to the new flat to carry on unpacking. They'd brought the bed from Paolo's old place. It was in pieces on the floor. Paolo put it back together and tried not to count the hours until Luis came home and they spent their first night in the riverside apartment block.

Days with Toni always wore Paolo out. Still missing the sofa, he stretched out on the bed under the pretence of watching the news. He dozed off before the headlines played out and woke sometime later to soft lips at his neck. "Hmm. Please tell me it's you and not that weirdo from downstairs letting himself in?"

Luis rumbled quietly and sank his teeth into the place that made Paolo squirm. "He wouldn't have needed to let himself in. You left the door open."

"Damn it. Toni promised he'd shut it."

"Don't blame him. You do that shit all the time."

Guilty as charged. Paolo was just grateful that Luis no longer felt the need to triple lock the doors every night before he could sleep. That he *did* sleep, like a man who was loved and safe, and that he woke slowly every morning with the sun instead of jumping awake with fear in his eyes. Paolo was grateful for everything about Luis, even the parts that still made his heart ache with sadness, a feeling that was a million miles away while Luis had his lips on Paolo's neck.

They'd fucked a lot in the last six months, but Luis still found ways to surprise him. He stripped Paolo naked and then himself, revealing every inch of lovely tattooed skin as Paolo licked his lips, and slowly jerked his lubed cock. "What do you want? You want me to fuck you?"

Luis shook his head and climbed over Paolo, straddling him before easing himself down, impaling himself on Paolo's dick with a low, tortured groan. "I want it like this."

Paolo let out a shaky breath. "Then have it. Take what you want from me."

Luis moved with a grace that brought Paolo to the edge in just a few rolls of his hips. He squeezed and clenched, and Paolo moaned as sensation rocked him. "Fuck, you're so bad for my stamina."

Eyes rolling, Luis fucked himself harder, faster, and the bed squeaked in protest.

Paolo groaned again, and Luis bent to kiss him.

"I can hear you," he whispered. "You know? Like we said? I kept it in so I could hear you."

"Yeah? You wanna hear me come?"

"Yeah, fuck yeah. I wanna hear it."

Paolo bent his legs and gripped Luis's shoulder. He thrust up, claiming the rough rhythm Luis had set, and slammed into him, shouting as the pleasure already sluicing through him ramped up. There was zero chance of him keeping Luis waiting.

Between them, Luis's dick slid along Paolo's abdomen, trapped in a vortex of friction that made Luis get loud too. Paolo started to come, and he pressed up into Luis and stayed there as his body shook and trembled. He whispered filth in Luis's ear, and Luis came with a wild yell, wet warmth spurting onto Paolo's belly.

They came down slowly, Luis rocking his hips until the very last moment, drawing every gasp and groan from Paolo, only stopping when Paolo had nothing left. Then they lay together, naked and entwined, and it didn't matter that Luis had heard it a thousand times, Paolo still needed to say it.

He pushed Luis's crazy hair back from his sweaty face and kissed his jaw, his cheek, his lips. "I love you."

Luis smiled, happy and carefree. "I know. I love you too."

PATREON

Not ready to let go of Luis and Paolo? Or looking for sneak peeks at future books in the series? Alternative POVs, outtakes, and missing moments from **all** Garrett's books can be found on her Patreon site. Misfits, Slide, Strays...the works. Because you know what? Garrett wasn't ready to let her boys go either.

Pledges start from as little as $2, and all content is available at the lowest tier.

NEWSLETTER

For the most up to date news and free books, subscribe to my newsletter HERE.

This is a zero spam zone. Maximum number of emails you will receive is one per month.

LUCKY — A SHORT EXCERPT

Dom

"In point two miles, the destination is on your left."

I shuddered; excitement and dread battled for space in my screwed-up soul. *This fucking place.* There was something about downtown Dalston I could never escape, even when months and months passed between visits. Maybe it was the smell—the Turkish restaurants, and the grotty meat market. Sizzling chargrilled lamb mixed with raw chicken flesh that was well past its best.

Or perhaps it was the haze that descended on me every time I cruised the streets, searching out an address I'd tapped into my GPS, cut and pasted from Grindr. The brutal tunnel vision that wouldn't lift until I'd paid someone to drain me dry.

Yeah, that's right. 'Cause it wasn't enough to chase down a stranger on a hook-up app, I was going to pay that motherfucker too—for his time, his silence...for the privilege of indulgence.

I rolled down my blacked-out window and another shiver passed through me. Indulgence. Something else I couldn't seem to escape. In my world, it was a lifestyle, a given...even now, when every part of me, except my dick, was screaming at me to turn my souped-up wank mobile round and go home.

But I didn't go home. I squinted at the numbers and names on the blocks of flats and parked my car in the street next to the one I wanted, 'cause I was a fucking ninja at this shit, and knew by now to keep hook ups as far away from my car as humanly possible.

"Nice wheels. You some kind of billionaire?"

I shivered again at the memory. Not quite, but the attention was dangerous, so I avoided it...like I avoided everything else.

Dickhead.

I locked my car and took the long way back to the nondescript block of flats I needed. Crossed the road a few times. Lingered outside a dodgy chicken shop and pretended to talk native on the phone.

Fucking charade. But it calmed my nerves. Like putting on a show for the people around me who couldn't give two shits what I was doing in their postcode could make everything right.

The block of flats was dodgier than I'd expected. My hook up—LCK£_98—buzzed me inside, and I jogged up the grimy stairs to the type of landing I hadn't seen since my mum sold her Thetford council place for big bucks a decade ago. Back then places like this had been home. Now it felt like I'd been dropped on the moon.

I wandered the corridor until I came to a grubby front door. There were no numbers on it, but powers of deduction led me to believe it was the right one.

That and the fact that it was on the latch—left open for any old closeted queer to stroll in.

I shut the door behind me, hard enough to announce my arrival, and hopefully convince whoever was behind that profile picture that I wasn't a fucking target. I'd survived a dozen Grindr encounters, but rocking up at some rando's house didn't get any easier.

Footsteps sounded from within the flat, and nerves started a new rave in my stomach. I glanced at the stained walls and broken floorboards. By now I'd had my dick sucked in worse places, but the vibe tickling my belly right now was ambiguous enough to kick-start my already-thumping heart.

"Wow. You're not what I was expecting."

I jumped and whirled around to face a doorway I hadn't noticed to my left. Blinked. And did that shit all over again. *Fucking hell. Are you kidding me?* LCK£_98's profile picture had been a pale, slim torso, and in our private message exchange he'd sent me a snap of his full lips pressed together in a teasing pout, but there'd been nothing else to giveaway the streak of fae-like beauty that stood before me now. Dark skinny jeans clung to his long legs, and a ripped vest hung from his slender frame, showing swathes of milky skin, all set off by piercing blue eyes, a ton of weathered leather bracelets, and sandy hair tied into a messy knot at the nape of his neck.

Long hair was my kryptonite. *Damn. Did I dream him?*

BUY OR BORROW LUCKY HERE

#BLM - UNSUNG HEROES OF ROMANCE

I've never read a book by a WOC author in our genre that didn't make me weep with how damn good it is. Below is a list of some of my faves, but there are many *many* more to be found.

Scars and Secrets, by Avril Ashton
Something About You, by Riley Hart
Take Care of You, by Gianni Holmes
Work For It, by Talia Hibbert
Love's Changes, by La Quette
Defined by Deceit, by A.E. Via

ABOUT THE AUTHOR

Bonus Material available for all books on Garrett's Patreon account. Includes short stories from Misfits, Slide, Strays, What Remains, Dream, and much more. Sign up here: https://www.patreon.com/garrettleigh

Facebook Fan Group, Garrett's Den... https://www.facebook.com/groups/garre...

Garrett Leigh is an award-winning British writer, cover artist, and book designer. Her debut novel, Slide, won Best Bisexual Debut at the 2014 Rainbow Book Awards, and her polyamorous novel, Misfits was a finalist in the 2016 LAMBDA awards, and was again a finalist in 2017 with Rented Heart.

In 2017, she won the EPIC award in contemporary romance with her military novel, Between Ghosts, and the contemporary romance category in the Bisexual Book Awards with her novel What Remains.

When not writing, Garrett can generally be found procrastinating on Twitter, cooking up a storm, or sitting on her behind doing as little as possible, all the while shouting at her menagerie of children and animals and attempting to tame her unruly and wonderful FOX.

Garrett is also an award winning cover artist, taking the silver medal at the Benjamin Franklin Book Awards in 2016. She designs for various publishing houses and independent authors at blackjazzdesign.com, and co-owns the specialist stock site moonstockphotography.com

Connect with Garrett
www.garrettleigh.com

Printed in Great Britain
by Amazon